Customer Service:
The Key to Winning Lifetime Customers

Written by Marian Thomas
Edited by National Seminars Publications

NATIONAL SEMINARS PUBLICATIONS
6901 West 63rd Street • P.O. Box 2949 • Shawnee Mission, Kansas 66201-1349
1-800-258-7246 • 1-913-432-7757

Customer Service: *The Key to Winning Lifetime Customers*
Published by National Seminars Publications
© 1989 National Seminars Publications

Printed in the United States of America

1 2 3 4 5 6 7 8 9 10

ISBN 1-55852-029-5

Table of Contents

1
THE MOVE TO A
SERVICE ECONOMY

". . . service people are the most important ones
in the organization.
Without them there is no product, no sale, and no profit.
Indeed, they are the product."

J.W. Marriott, Jr.
Chairman of the Board and President
Marriott Corporation[1]

Over the last several years, America has shifted from a manufacturing-based economy to a service-based economy. In fact, more than three-quarters of all jobs created in this country in the last decade have been in the service industry.

Service accounts for an estimated 60 percent of the gross national

[1] From the foreword by J.W. Marriott, Jr., *At America's Service*, by Karl Albrecht (Homewood, Ill: Dow Jones-Irwin, 1988).

product and 70 percent of all jobs in the United States. It is a vital part of our economy and an important factor in the success of companies today.

Regardless of the product or service, generally customers can choose to do business with several different companies. Most of these will offer similar products at comparable prices. Often, the only thing that separates one company from another is service.

As the front-line person in your company who deals with customers on a day-to-day basis, your job — perhaps more than any other — influences the way the customer perceives your company. From the customer's point-of-view, you *are* the company. If you are friendly and helpful, the company is perceived as a pleasant and easy place to do business. By the same token, if you are surly and uncooperative, the company is perceived as unfriendly and a place where it is difficult to get what you want.

Based on your attitude and actions, customers will make a judgment on:

- What kind of people the company employs.

- The company's value system.

- Whether or not the company practices what it preaches in its advertising.

Customer Service Defined

As a customer service employee for your company, you may be responsible for one or more of the following functions: sales, service or problem-solving.

- **Sales.** You are responsible for selling your company's tangible or intangible products. The sales process may take place in person or through telephone contact.

- **Service.** Customers come to your company when they need a particular service. This can involve sales or it can involve filling an order for a customer. For example, if you work for a travel agency, your job is to book customers' travel plans.

- **Problem-Solving.** Customers come to you with problems they have experienced in dealing with your company, and it's your job to find a solution. For example, a customer brings you a radio that was purchased in your store which has stopped working. It is your job, through interaction with the customer, to determine an equitable solution: refund the customer's money, replace the item or exchange it for another brand of radio.

Regardless of which role you perform, your main goal is to develop good customer relationships.

Facts About Customer Service

Research shows that, generally, most people feel good about the products they purchase, but they are not so happy with the service they receive. As a customer service employee, you can change that. If you want to get some perspective on exactly how valuable your job is, consider these facts:

• Ninety-six percent of unhappy customers never let a business know that they are unhappy.

• For every complaint received by a company, there are actually 26 customers with problems, six of which are serious.

• Customers who complain about a problem, even if it is not resolved, are more likely to do business with the company again than those who don't voice their complaints.

• Fifty-four to 70 percent of customers who voice their complaints will do business with the organization in the future if they feel their complaint has been resolved. That figure jumps to 95 percent if the customer feels the complaint has been resolved promptly.

• On the average, a customer who has a problem with a company will tell nine or 10 other people about it. By the same token, he will tell only four of five other people about a good experience.

• A customer who complains about a problem but has it resolved tells five people about the treatment he received.

• If a business loses one customer who normally spends $50 a week, it will experience a $949,000 reduction in sales the following year.

- A business will spend five times as much to acquire a new customer as it does to service an existing one.

How does all of this affect you? First, happy customers mean a more profitable company and that in turn translates into job security for you. But even more importantly, developing good customer service skills will help you work more effectively with your customers and provide you with greater job satisfaction.

Customer Service Is Everybody's Business

The old school of thought was that customer service was the responsibility of the customer service representative or the complaint department. In today's service-driven economy, however, companies have come to realize that customer service is *everyone's* business. Every individual in a company is either serving a customer or serving someone whose job it is to serve the customer.

In order to do the best possible job of serving the customer, it's important that you work well with your fellow employees. That means being a good team player. Further information on how you can work as part of the customer service team is included in Chapter 7 of this handbook.

What You Will Learn From This Handbook

Working effectively with customers is not a trait you are born with, it is a skill you must learn. Although it is true that some people are naturally better at working with the public than others, everyone can learn how to communicate with customers and how to help them meet their needs. The key to success in your job is knowing what your customers expect, how to keep them happy and how to deal with them.

As a customer service employee, you come in contact with hundreds of people every day. It can be a challenging, rewarding job or you can find it difficult and impossible. How you view your job will depend on your attitude and the skills you develop to do it better.

As in any job, your attitude about your work will also affect other areas of your life. Therefore, it is important that you are happy with what you do. If your experiences with customers are positive, you will have a positive outlook on your job, and it will affect your overall satisfaction with your life. If, on the other hand, they are negative, they will cloud your overall perspective.

Through this handbook you will learn:

• Techniques for dealing with customers.

• What customers want.

• How to communicate effectively with customers.

• How to handle special customers and those with complaints.

• How to keep customers happy.

• How to work with your fellow employees to make sure that the customer's experience is pleasant.

• The function of the customer service supervisor.

2

WHAT CUSTOMERS EXPECT

Providing good service is not enough. In order for a transaction to be successful, the customer must *perceive* that he is receiving good service.

Customers come to you because they have a need. It's up to you to determine what that need is and then meet it according to their expectations.

Customers will remain loyal to your company as long as they believe that the level of service being offered meets their needs. If, however, they believe the level of service no longer satisfies those needs, they will go elsewhere.

Looking at the Big Picture

Your customers are concerned with finding solutions to their problems or having their needs met. Because of this, they have a much broader view of your company than you do. Your view is probably fairly limited to what happens in your department. As a result, your view of the company and your customers' view can sometimes be in conflict.

In order to serve your customers' needs adequately, it's important for you to guard against tunnel vision. Get to know your organization — the entire organization. This is the only way you can truly help your customers achieve their goals. The best way to learn about the organization is to visit other departments and talk with your fellow employees. Learn what they do and what their jobs entail. This information will be useful when you have to interact with them to get a customer's problem solved.

Let's look at an example. Say you are a bank teller. A customer brings you a check for $100 and wants to cash it. You check your records and discover that he has only $50 in his account. You explain that you are unable to cash the check because there are insufficient funds to cover it. The customer, on the other hand, claims to have deposited $1,000 in the account the day before and demands to know where it is.

Technically, you have done your job. But just telling the customer that he can't have the money is not helping him find a solution to his problem. Your main concern should be to help the customer find out what happened to his $1,000 deposit. If you are familiar with other departments in the bank, you can check on the status of the deposit quickly. And, rather than frustrating the customer, you can provide him with specific answers.

If you need to, call on your supervisor for guidance in these situations. But, be careful not to completely turn the problem over to him. You will be much better off if you use your supervisor strictly as a resource person and follow through on your own. If you do, you will gain the respect of the customer and save your supervisor time.

What Customers Want From You

What do customers want? Before you read any further, close the book and write down five or six qualities that you think your customers want. Then, reopen the book and continue reading. See how your perspective of what customers want matches what studies have shown they are looking for.

Overall, customers want to be treated fairly and courteously. Here are some other essential qualities that they look for in a service experience:

- **Courtesy.** This sounds basic, but many customers have been lost due to rude service people. As an individual involved in customer contact, it's important for you to leave your problems and your bad moods at the door. Bringing them to work only creates more problems. When a customer walks into your store or calls you on the telephone, he wants to feel welcome. For your part, this involves greeting him enthusiastically, making him feel important and being helpful.

• **Prompt attention.** Nobody likes to wait or feel as though they are being ignored. How many times have you waited at a checkout counter and began to wonder if anyone was going to take your money? If a customer is left "cooling his heels" while the customer service employee chats with co-workers or attends to other non-customer related details, the customer feels unimportant. If you are busy when a customer walks up, simply look up, smile and say, "I'll be with you in just a minute."

• **Reliability.** Customers want their shopping experience to be as hassle-free as possible. They want to know that when they walk into your store or company, they will find what they want or get an answer to their question. They also expect that, if you make a promise, you will keep it. And, if you are unable to, you will let them know ahead of time so they won't be inconvenienced.

• **Personal attention.** No one likes to feel like a number. And, with today's technology, that can sometimes be a problem. Remember the last time you received a letter in the mail which was obviously a copy and addressed, "Dear Friend"? Chances are you didn't even read it. But, when was the last time you threw out a letter that was obviously an original and began, "Dear Mr. Smith," or "Dear Tom"?

We all like personal attention. It makes us feel important and that makes us feel good. As a customer service employee, you can show a customer personal attention by addressing him by his name and by discussing with him at length what he needs.

• **Responsiveness.** Customers like to feel as though their business is appreciated. And that's exactly what a customer service employee tells customers when he responds to their needs enthusiastically. If a customer is ignored, he feels as though his business is not appreciated, and he will take it elsewhere.

• **Knowledgeable staff.** Customers expect customer service employees to be knowledgeable about the products they are selling. In today's high technology and deregulated industries, customers must rely on service employees to help them make choices. For example, a customer calling a travel agent relies heavily on the agent's knowledge to ensure that he is getting the best price on an airline ticket.

• **Empathy.** Customers want to be understood. This is particularly true when there is a problem. If the customer service employee acts as though he could care less, the customer will leave feeling that the company doesn't care about its customers. When a customer explains a problem he is having, respond by saying, "I understand why you might feel that way . . . "

• **Tangibles.** You may not be able to tell a book by its cover, but customers believe you can tell a store by its surroundings. Clean, attractive facilities and well-groomed employees reflect positively on the company. As a service employee, it is important for you to keep your area neat and clean, and dress in a manner that projects the kind of image your company wants to convey.

What Customers Want From a Sales Perspective

As a service employee, you may be involved in sales, problem-solving or service. If you are in sales, there are basically four things a customer needs to know from you:

1. The cost of a product or service.

2. How it works, including what benefits the customer can expect to receive.

3. The pros and cons of different options.

4. Various payment options available.

If you leave out any of these elements, you are not responding to your customer's needs. As a service employee in a sales position, your job is to find what the customer needs or wants and then show how your product or service fills those needs. To do this, you must go beyond the basic concept of ringing up the sale.

Selling a customer a product or service he doesn't need or want is only going to cause you problems down the road. The customer will either return it or, worse yet, keep it and not shop at your store again. Either way you lose. The company loses future sales, and you lose the confidence and trust of a customer.

Determining what it is that a customer wants is not always easy. Some people come in knowing exactly what they want; others have no idea. Still others *think* they know what they want when actually they don't. It's your job to question them thoroughly to get the information you need to help them. Tips on how you can do this will be explained in depth in Chapter 3.

What Motivates Customers to Buy

Many people presume that price is the most important motivator for most people when making a buying decision. But studies show that customer service is actually the deciding factor. In a study of 2,374 customers, more than 40 percent said that poor service was the reason they switched to the competition while only eight percent listed price as a contributing factor. In another study, 60 percent of those questioned said having needs met is more important than price.

Your main function is to meet the customer's need. Therefore, it is important for you to understand some of the psychological reasons why customers buy. Here are some factors that motivate people to buy.

- **Need.** The customer needs a product or service to solve a problem, make a job easier or otherwise help him in some way. Determining what that need is and then helping the customer find the right product or service to fulfill it is the key with these individuals.

- **Personal gratification.** People who shop for personal gratification feel a sense of power when they buy. They often wish to dominate the service transaction. Let them lead the way.

- **Self-improvement.** These individuals are looking for a product or service that will help improve their life or lifestyle. Talk about how the product will help them and you reinforce their judgment, thus making the buying decision easier.

- **Involvement in the process.** These are people who like to go to self-service gas stations and box grocery stores. They like to become involved in the sales process. You can win their loyalty by encouraging them to be an active participant in the transaction.

- **For status.** Some people buy certain products for the prestige. If you can determine this up front, you can use it to your advantage in making a sale.

- **To help others.** People who are buying presents for others or picking up items to help out a friend appreciate all the help they can get. If you can save them time, you will create a loyal customer.

• **For the fun of it.** You've seen the bumper stickers that say, "Born To Shop." Some people actually feel that way. They get great enjoyment out of shopping. If you share their enthusiasm, you will make more sales with these people.

• **Because it's their job.** Some people have to make purchases because it is part of their job. If you help them find quality items at a good price, they will look good to their employers, and you, in turn, will gain their loyalty.

What Customers Want From a Service Perspective

When selling a product, you are selling a tangible. When you provide or sell a service, you are selling an intangible. For example, if you work for XYZ Widget company, customers come to you to find the exact widget they need. If, on the other hand, you work for XYZ Hairstyling, your customers will come to you looking for a cut and shave.

When you sell or provide a service, it is crucial that you determine the customer's wants and needs because customer satisfaction will be heavily dependent on how closely you meet the customer's expectations. If you are a hair stylist, for example, you wouldn't dream of cutting a customer's hair without first finding out what style he wanted. You would also discuss price to ensure that he knew how much he was paying and what he would get for his money.

Conclusion

In determining what customers are looking for, try to view the experience through their eyes. How would you want to be treated? What would you expect? Use your own experiences with other service industries to help you create the kind of atmosphere that makes a customer want to come back.

3

EFFECTIVE COMMUNICATION

Communication is fundamental to your job as a customer service employee. In fact, it has been estimated that more than half of your job consists of communication.

In order to be effective, you have to communicate with customers, co-workers, other departments and sometimes even vendors outside of your company. As we discussed earlier, it doesn't matter how good a job you do, the important thing is how the customer perceives the job you are doing.

Communication is a two-way sharing of information that results in an understanding between the receiver and the sender. If both don't have the same understanding of the message, they are not truly communicating. Communication is the key to how you are perceived.

Communication Breakdowns

Communication between two people can break down when emotions, attitudes, nonverbal clues, role expectations or the wrong choice of words get in the way.

• **Emotions.** Strong emotions can sometimes cause a listener to tune out. For example, if a customer comes to you and says, "You did this *all* wrong," your first response is to be angry. If you concentrate on the anger instead of encouraging the customer to explain what the problem is, you won't come any closer to solving the problem.

• **Attitude.** Attitudes are expressed by the way you act, look and demonstrate feelings. If you convey a negative attitude, it affects what the person hears. For example, if you adopt a superior attitude, the listener is going to concentrate on your air of superiority and not hear what you are actually saying. If, for example, your response on the above example was, "Well dear, here's the problem. It's *obvious* . . .," the individual will probably be so intent on the superior, sarcastic attitude you are conveying that he won't even hear your response.

• **Nonverbal clues.** How you stand, how you dress and even the expression on your face all affect how you communicate. For example, if you work in a jewelry store and come dressed in jeans and a t-shirt, your customers will probably not take you seriously. They will be so busy looking at the way you're dressed, they won't hear all the wonderful things you say about the diamond ring in your hand — no matter how knowledgeable you are. Your appearance can also devalue the quality of the merchandise in the eyes of the customer.

• **Role expectations.** This involves how others expect you to act. If you do not come across in the manner they anticipate, they may become distracted, thus breaking down communication. For example, if you are introduced by a fellow employee as an expert in widgets and then you can't answer their simplest questions, they are going to find it difficult to communicate with you. This type of communication problem can also create a negative impression of the company you work for as well as the products or services you offer.

• **Choice of words.** The words you choose to communicate your message can sometimes cause a communications breakdown. Choose your words carefully. Let's look at an example of how words can make a difference.

Customer:	"I would like to get a refund."
Customer Service Employee:	"We can't refund your money for that merchandise *now*. If you didn't want it, you should have returned it within 30 days like our policy states."

There are several things wrong with the above response. First, the employee uses negative phrases which are bound to put the customer on the defensive: "can't," "didn't want" and "should have."

Second, he says, "If you didn't want it . . ." Does he know for a fact that the customer didn't want it, or is he making an assumption? Finally, he throws the policy manual in the customer's face without even knowing if the customer was made aware of the policy.

A much more effective way to handle the situation would be to say, "May I ask why you are returning this merchandise? Let me tell you what I can do. I can give you a voucher in the amount of the purchase which you can use to buy anything else in the store. Is that satisfactory?"

Verbal Communication

When you talk to a customer you express yourself both verbally and nonverbally. Both can have an effect on your message. Here are some tips on making the most of your verbal communication.

- **Greet the customer warmly.** Extend your hand and wear a smile. This will make the customer feel welcome and get your transaction off to a good start.

- **Be precise.** Don't use phrases like, "I'll do my best." The customer has no idea what "your best" is. If you're dealing with a problem, he may think that your best is getting the problem resolved, when actually your best may only be finding out why the mistake happened.

- **Don't leave out any details.** If you tell a customer that a product costs $20, that is what he is going to expect. If there are additional charges, be sure and let him know up front. For example, the product may cost $20, but if there is an additional $2 charge for taxes and a $5 charge for shipping and he doesn't know it, then he will be upset.

- **Think before you speak.** The more you know about the customer, the better you can serve him. If you think about what you're going to say before you start talking, you'll be better able to get your message across.

- **Use small talk sparingly.** It's okay to engage in a little small talk to break the ice, but don't let it distract you from your original goal: to help the customer find what he needs.

Nonverbal Communication

Nonverbal messages affect the way you communicate. In fact, experts say that nonverbal communication accounts for half of what we communicate, whereas, tone of voice accounts for 40 percent and the actual words only 10 percent. So, you can see how important nonverbal messages are in communication.

What are nonverbal messages? Anything you do that distracts or enhances what you are saying. Your smile, posture, dress and gestures are all examples of nonverbal communication. They can work for you or against you.

For example, if you dress professionally, customers will be more apt to think of you, and treat you, as a professional. They will give credence to what you say even before you open your mouth.

If you slouch, customers will interpret it as a lack of self-confidence and presume you are not knowledgeable about the product, even though you may know it backward and forward. Think about the nonverbal clues you give. Are you saying, "Hi, I'm a knowledgeable professional, and I want to help you," or are you giving the impression that you are indifferent to your job and the customer?

Evaluate your nonverbal messages carefully and make sure you're projecting the image you want to get across.

Listening

An important part of communicating is listening. Listening involves more than what you hear with your ears. It involves what you hear with your mind. You may hear the words, but unless you really listen to what is being said, you won't be able to respond to the customer's request.

Like speaking, listening is a skill that can be learned. Many people have a hard time listening because they allow themselves to be distracted. If you can break yourself of that habit, you will become a much better listener.

Becoming distracted when someone is speaking is easy. Studies show that the average person speaks at a rate of approximately 125 words per minute. However, we have the ability to process what we hear at the rate of about 500 words a minute. The result is that sometimes the brain gets bored and starts concentrating on other things. We've all experienced it. You are sitting in a crowded auditorium listening to a speech. The next thing you know everybody is clapping, and you suddenly realize that you don't know what the speaker said. (You may, however, have your entire menu for that night's dinner planned out in your mind.)

If you would like to improve your listening skills, try the following techniques:

1. **Listen for facts and feelings.** People express themselves with both facts ("The tape recorder that I bought from you broke during a major interview.") and feelings ("And I'm very upset because I missed my deadline."). What this person is doing is stating the fact that the tape recorder is broken and expressing his feelings of anger and disappointment. In developing a response you have to address both. Your response to this situation might be, "I'm sorry this happened. I'm sure it caused you some anxiety and inconvenience. Let me get you a new one, and we will try it out to make sure it works before you leave the store."

2. **Become actively involved in the conversation.** Don't just sit back and listen without any kind of response. If you understand what the individual is saying, let him know by nodding your head or by saying, "Yes, I understand." If you don't, stop him and ask for clarification.

3. **Don't be distracted.** Don't let other employees, customers or things going on around you steal your attention. If you're not giving the customer your total attention, you're bound to miss an important point. Customers can tell when you're distracted, and the message it conveys to them is that their problem or concern is not important to you.

4. **Wait until the customer finishes talking before formulating your response.** It's human nature to want to respond immediately. But often, we start thinking about what we're going to say before the individual finishes talking. Avoid answering too quickly. Make sure you don't miss anything the customer says. If you don't wait, you may miss out on important information that you need to respond effectively.

5. **Don't prejudge.** Don't let a customer's appearance distract you from what he has to say. If you look at an individual and decide that he can't afford your top-of-the-line product because of the way he is dressed, you may be missing out on an important sale. Looks can be deceiving. Consider the man who went into a luxury car dealership dressed in the clothes he works in around the house. One salesman sized him up quickly and concluded he couldn't afford one of the cars. Another salesman, however, decided to practice his selling skills and approached the man. Not only did the man buy a car for himself, but he later returned and bought one for his wife.

6. **Clarify what's been said.** Once the customer finishes telling you what he wants, restate his request to ensure that you fully understand. In doing so, be sure to use "I" statements. Say, "As I understand it, you would like the biggest widget we have," rather than, "You said you want the biggest widget we have." If that's not what the customer said, he will be irritated if he thinks he has been misquoted.

Listening is imperative for proper communication. If a customer feels he is not being listened to, he will begin to speak louder and become more emphatic. This can cause embarrassment and result in an unpleasant experience for both of you. Retain control of the situation at all times.

In communicating with the customer, find out what he really wants. Don't let him get by with making vague statements such as "I want to return this because it doesn't work." Saying it doesn't work may mean:

• It is broken and doesn't work.

• He doesn't know how to use it and can't get it to work.

• It doesn't fit his needs, and so it doesn't work for him in the specific application he had hoped it would.

• It doesn't work the way he thought it would.

As you can see in the above example, your response would be different in each scenario. It's up to you to probe and ask questions that will lead you to the real problem.

The Art of Questioning

Part of helping the customer get what he wants involves defining his exact needs. You have to listen to not only what the customer says, but also what he doesn't say. Sometimes customers have a hard time expressing themselves. When this happens, you have to get to the real issue by probing. As a customer service employee, you do this through questioning.

There are two basic types of questions you can ask: open and closed. Open questions are used as a springboard for discussion. Closed are used when all you want, or need, are "yes" and "no" answers. Using both types of questions helps you gain control of the conversation.

Use open questions to:

- Define problems.

- Establish needs.

- Understand requests.

- Get more information.

Use closed questions to:

- Get the customer to agree.

- Clarify what has been said.

- Summarize a conversation or confirm an order.

Communicating by Phone

When a customer calls on the telephone, you don't have the advantage of being able to read his nonverbal clues. Therefore, answering questions or solving problems over the phone involves different skills.

Just like in face-to-face contact, the way you greet the customer will set the tone for the conversation that follows. When answering phone calls, follow these four basic rules:

1. Greet the caller.

2. Give the name of your organization or department.

3. State your name.

4. Offer assistance.

For example, "Good Morning. This is John Smith in customer service. How may I help you?" Be enthusiastic and smile even before you pick up the receiver. The caller may not be able to see your smile, but he will hear it. Listen carefully to what the caller says. Most of the time, he will be calling to:

• Make a statement.

• Voice an objection.

• Ask a question.

If a customer voices an objection, address it immediately. Don't ignore it. For example, if the customer says, "I tried to buy the light bulbs that were on sale, and there weren't any left. I don't think you ever did have any of the advertised specials." You need to respond to the objection before you solve the problem. If the customer is correct and the store did not have the specials, explain why. "You're right Mr. Smith, we didn't have the light bulbs. When we placed our ad, the shipment was scheduled to arrive in time for the sale. However, a snowstorm detained it. I will be happy to send you a rain check so you can get the light bulbs at the advertised price. I will also send you a post card and let you know when the light bulbs are in stock."

Be careful not to confuse a statement and an objection. If you do, you may get sidetracked trying to counter the objection and lose control of the conversation. For example, a customer may say, "The claims your product makes are unbelievable." Depending on how he says it, he may mean the claims are false, the product doesn't work as promised or that the claims are exciting. If you begin to defend the product, you may never find out why he actually called. If you have any doubts about what the customer is saying, ask an open-ended question to get more information. For instance, "Unbelievable? In what way?"

Here are some tips for dealing effectively with customers on the phone.

• **Make sure you understand all the features of your phone.**
Nothing is more irritating than to be put on hold and suddenly hear a dial tone. If you're uncertain how to use the features, ask your supervisor or a fellow employee to explain them *before* you get a customer on the line.

- **Answer the phone as quickly as possible.** The standard rule of thumb in a business is to answer the phone within three rings. Customers will develop an impression of you and your company by the number of times they have to listen to the phone ring.

- **Hold the mouthpiece in front of your mouth and speak clearly.** If the mouthpiece is off to the side, your comments will sound garbled. Speak clearly and in an audible tone. Avoid making the customer strain in order to hear you.

- **Avoid unnecessary noise.** Don't wear jewelry that is constantly banging into the phone, have a radio on nearby, or shuffle papers. It is very distracting to the caller.

- **Don't talk with others while on a call.** If you do, the customer will feel like you are not giving his request or problem your full attention. You won't be able to respond appropriately because you won't know what has been said.

- **Don't eat, drink or chew gum while talking on the phone.** This is not only distracting, but also rude.

- **Always use the hold button when you ask a customer to wait.** Don't just put the receiver down. Can you imagine how embarrassing it would be if an unsuspecting co-worker started talking about a subject not meant for the customer's ears, and it was overheard by the customer on the other end of the line?

- **Ask permission to place the caller on hold.** Don't say, "Hold please," and immediately depress the hold button. Ask if it is okay with the customer, and then wait for a response. Saying, "The other line is ringing, may I put you on hold for just a minute," is a much nicer way of handling the situation.

- **Don't leave a customer hanging on hold.** If you must put a customer on hold, don't leave him there for an inappropriate amount of time. It is common business practice not to leave a customer on hold any longer than one minute. If you can't find the information you need or get an answer to his question in that amount of time, ask for a phone number and tell him you will call back, giving the approximate time. "I can have an answer for you within 10 minutes," or "I can get back to you later this afternoon," makes the customer feel more in control of the situation.

When You Have to Say "No"

Unfortunately, you won't always be able to do what the customer wants. You can, however, make the experience less frustrating for him if you follow a few simple rules:

- **Explain why it can't be done.** Don't just say you can't do it. Give details. Explain why you can't do what the customer has requested.

- **Don't quote policy.** Tell the underlying reasons why. For example, don't say, "Our policy won't allow me to give you your money back without a receipt." Instead say, "I can't give you your money back for this sweater because our winter merchandise has all been sold, therefore we can't put it back on the rack."

- **Don't patronize.** There is nothing more frustrating to a customer than being talked down to. Keep your comments on a professional, adult level.

- **Offer alternatives.** Don't just say no, try to help the customer find a solution to his problem. Using the example above, you might say, "I can't give you your money back, however, I can give you a credit voucher which you can use to buy other merchandise in the store."

- **Concentrate on the positives.** Don't dwell on the negatives. For example, instead of saying, "I can't help you," say "Here is what I can do." This approach will convince the customer that you are trying to help him.

Express Yourself

Sometimes it's not *what* you say but *how* you say it. Review these sample statements to determine ways you can improve *how* you say *what* you say.

- **Avoid making excuses.** Saying, "I'm sorry, but as you can see we are pretty backlogged," isn't going to impress the customer. He will probably feel that you didn't think his order was important enough to give it priority. Instead say, "I'm sorry your order hasn't been processed yet. Let me see what happened." This personalizes the response and lets the customer know that you will try to find a solution.

- **Eliminate phrases such as "you will have to."** Command statements such as these tend to make the customer defensive and give him the feeling that he is being put off. Instead of saying, "I can't help you with that. You'll have to talk to someone in our shipping department," you might say something like, "May I transfer you to our shipping department? They will be able to trace your shipment and tell you when you can expect it." This helps the customer feel like he is in control.

- **Don't point the finger at other employees.** Making such accusations makes you look less than professional and gives the customer the feeling that the people within your company don't work well together. It also makes him wonder whether or not he will get his problem resolved. A better way to state it would be, "According to my records you should have received your order by now. Let me call our shipping department to see if there is a reason why it hasn't arrived." This makes the customer feel like you work with others in your company to get problems resolved quickly.

- **Avoid making non-specific statements.** Customers who are told that the salesperson "will try" or "will do their best" may become suspicious of just how hard he'll try. The customer may believe that what the customer service employee is actually saying is that he will go through the motions, but won't necessarily make a sincere effort on the part of the customer.

- **Don't give unnecessary details.** The customer doesn't need to know that Mr. Smith can't help him because he is at the doctor. Simply say, "Mr. Smith is not in right now. May I have him call you, or can I help you?" Also avoid statements like, "I don't know where Mr. Smith is. I guess he is still out to lunch." These kinds of statements make Mr. Smith look irresponsible and your entire company look bad.

- **Avoid the phrase "should be."** Don't tell a customer that the technician "should be there within an hour," unless you are certain that he will arrive by then. The customer will expect him to be there. If the technician doesn't arrive within an hour, the customer will be upset with you for leading him on, and the technician for not showing up when he was "supposed to."

- **Don't mention other complaints.** Avoiding making statements like, "He can't help you right now. He is handling another complaint," or "I'm sure we can do something. Another customer had the same problem last week." These kinds of statements lead the customer to believe that your company has a lot of complaints, and that's not the message you want to convey.

Conclusion

Communication is an important part of your job. If you do it effectively, you make your company look good. If you don't, you will look bad and so will your company.

Effective communication involves both speaking and listening skills. It is not something you are born knowing how to do. They are skills you have to acquire through practice. Learn them and they will serve you well.

4

HANDLING DIFFICULT OR SPECIAL CUSTOMERS

Basically, all customers want the same thing — good service. But, every once in a while, you will come across a customer who requires special treatment. Knowing how to handle these individuals will help make your job a little easier.

Here are some tips on dealing with special cases.

The Angry Customer

When angry customers call or come into your store or company, they have two messages they want to deliver: one has to do with facts, and the other has to do with their feelings. It's up to you to get past the feelings so you can get the facts you need to solve their problems.

In dealing with an angry customer, don't deny his anger. Telling a customer, "There's really no reason to get upset," is only going to make him *angrier*.

Here are some ways you can defuse an angry customer.

- **Keep your emotions in check.** Don't allow yourself to lose control. Determine the overall objective of the complaint (i.e. getting the customer a refund, finding the product he is looking for) and concentrate on it, not the customer's angry words.

- **Don't allow yourself to get defensive.** When you get defensive, it means you are becoming emotionally involved. You act like the customer is attacking you personally. Stay objective and emotionally detached.

- **Look beyond the anger.** Often what you are seeing is the individual's frustration that is brought on by unrelated problems. His anger may not have anything to do with the problem he is experiencing with your company. It may involve external factors such as personal problems: a flat tire or an argument with his boss. If you remember that there are often other forces at work, you will deal more effectively with an angry customer.

- **Anticipate potentially volatile situations.** Most of the time you can anticipate some of the things that are likely to make a customer angry. If possible, avoid these situations. For example, telling a customer that there is nothing you can do will generally upset him. Take a positive approach and say, "Let me see what I can do."

  Customers also get annoyed when they are shuffled around from department to department whether they are on the phone or standing in your store or office. Make every attempt to handle the problem yourself. If you can't, explain what needs to be done, who the customer needs to talk to, etc. Help make the process as easy as possible for the customer (help him fill out forms or personally take him to another office or department).

  If the customer is on the telephone, take his name and number before you transfer him. Also, tell him who he will be talking with. Stay on the line if possible until the transfer has been made.

- **Defuse the anger.** Try to get the customer past his anger. This will make it easier for you to find a solution to his problem. Let the customer blow off steam. Then try to find things the two of you can agree on. This will help you find an acceptable solution to the problem.

- **Don't make promises you can't keep.** Don't let a customer get you to make a promise in the heat of the moment that you can't keep. It will only cause you problems in the future.

- **Be sympathetic.** Indifference will send a customer out the door faster than failing to solve the problem. In fact, studies show that 68 percent of customers stop doing business with a company because of indifferent treatment by their employees. This compares to 14 percent who leave because of product dissatisfaction, and nine percent who leave because of competition. Listen carefully to what the customer has to say and let him know that you understand. For example, you might say, "I understand that this can be very frustrating. Let me see what I can do to help resolve this problem."

  Don't, however, agree with the customer if he begins criticizing the company. This approach will get you nowhere. You will lose the respect of the customer, and if your company finds out what you have said, you may lose your job.

- **Analyze the problem.** When customers are angry, they often don't express the real problem clearly. They are so intent on making sure that you understand their anger, they may forget to communicate some vital information that will help you solve the problem. As a customer service employee, it is your responsibility to uncover the exact problem and help the customer find a solution. Ask probing questions and repeat what the customer has said to make sure you understand fully.

- **Stress what you can do, not what you can't.** A response of "Let me see what I can do to help you," will defuse a customer's anger a lot faster than "I don't know what we can do about this."

- **Negotiate a solution.** Ask the customer how he would like the problem resolved. If it is within the realm of your authority and it is a reasonable request, do it. If not, negotiate a solution that both the customer and your company will be happy with.

- **Act on the problem.** Acting on the problem involves more than simply saying that you will take care of it. If there are several problems, set priorities and attack the most critical ones first. For example, if you are a travel agent and your customer calls to say that he is stuck in Tanzania because the airline you booked him on has just declared bankruptcy, find him a flight home first, then work on getting a refund.

- **Identify any potential problems that may arise.** If a customer is returning merchandise, for example, and you tell him that a credit will appear on his statement, tell him *which* statement. The customer may not realize that the closing date on his account has already passed. If the credit doesn't show up on his next statement, he will be calling you back. By explaining when he can expect the credit, you keep the customer happy and reduce the likelihood of getting another angry call.

- **Follow through.** Just because you have found a solution to the problem doesn't mean the problem has been solved. It's up to you to follow through and make certain that what you have promised actually happens. If it doesn't, you are bound to face another confrontation with the customer. For example, if a customer returns a defective item and you promise that credit will be issued on his account, don't just write a request and hope it happens. Call the credit department to make sure this happens.

The Unhappy Customer

We all know them — individuals who walk around with chips on their shoulders. They walk into your store and make a statement such as, "I'm sure you don't have what I'm looking for." They don't necessarily have a problem with you or your company, their problem is with life in general.

You can't expect to change the unhappy customer, but you can make the situation as easy as possible and protect yourself from being dragged into a bad mood.

Show these people as much compassion and warmth as possible. Chances are you won't be able to improve their moods, but you can determine what exactly it is they are looking for and, as a result, help them find it.

The Argumentative Customer

These people thrive on arguments. If you tell them a sweater is white, they'll say it's black. They are aggressive and probably disagree with, or question, everything you say.

Your first instinct is to disagree and argue back. But don't allow yourself to fall into the trap. In dealing with these people, try the following techniques.

- **Speak softly.** If you speak loudly they will speak louder and louder and soon you will both be shouting at each other.

- **Ask their opinion.** Argumentative people like to feel they are in control. If you try to rob them of that control, they become more argumentative. If, on the other hand, you give them some control, they are liable to ease up. For example, instead of saying, "This stereo is the best buy," you might tell a customer about all of the options available and the price on a couple of different stereos and then ask him, "Which do you think is the best buy?"

- **Concentrate on points of agreement.** Look for things you both agree on and build your conversation around them. For example, "You like XYZ's brand of stereo. So do I. I feel they make a very reliable piece of equipment. Don't you agree?"

- **Take five.** If you allow yourself to become angry, excuse yourself briefly and regain your composure. If you don't think you can deal effectively with the customer, ask another customer service employee to take over.

The Talkative Customer

These individuals can eat up a lot of your time if you let them. They come in to buy a widget, and by the time they leave, you know their entire life story. If no other customers are around, it may not be a problem to take the time to listen, but if others are waiting, you need to move the talker along.

Try to keep in mind that the reason most of these people talk so much is because they are lonely. Don't brush them off. Show compassion and interest, but make it clear that you have to assist other customers.

The Flirt

Flirts can be either men or women. The entire time you are trying to help them, they keep making comments with double meanings and sexual innuendos. As they do, they watch you carefully to see if you react in any way.

The reaction of most customer service employees is to become embarrassed, defensive, or put them down. None of these techniques is particularly effective. The more embarrassed or upset you get, the more comments they make.

In dealing with these customers, remain professional at all times. Ignore their remarks and instead concentrate your efforts on helping them with the product or service they are seeking. After all, the sooner they find what they are looking for, the sooner they will leave.

The Non-Talker

It's like trying to pull teeth to get this customer to tell you what he is looking for. It may be because he honestly isn't sure, or it may be because he has a hard time expressing himself. Be patient. Make him feel relaxed. Don't ask questions that require elaborate answers. For example, you may say something like, "Well let's look at these two shirts. Between the two, which do you prefer? The blue one? That's my favorite too. It's more tailored, and it will give you a more distinguished look."

By doing this, you have made the customer feel comfortable, assured him that he has good taste and at the same time, you've gotten some idea about the style and color of shirt he prefers.

His body language will also give you a clue as to what he is thinking. His verbal response may be the same to every shirt you pick out for him, "Yeah," but his face will tell you if you are on the right track.

The Habitual Complainer

The habitual complainer doesn't like anything. The service is poor, the prices are too high . . . chances are even the design of the building is probably "all wrong." Don't let this individual discourage you or drag you down. Realize that this is just part of his personality.

When the habitual complainer calls, try to separate legitimate complaints from phoney ones. Avoid becoming defensive, regardless of what he says. Let him talk.

If the complaint is legitimate, take the necessary steps to correct it and, like you would with any other customer, apologize for the inconvenience.

One warning! Be careful not to assume that *everything* the complainer complains about is frivolous. Although he sets himself up for this kind of response by crying wolf, it's up to you as a professional to distinguish between the legitimate and frivolous complaints.

The Obnoxious or Rude Customer

If you realize what these people are really like, it may be easier for you to deal with them. Often, they come across as arrogant and totally self-assured. Underneath, however, they are lonely and insecure.

Your first thought in dealing with obnoxious people may be to become sarcastic or "put them in their place." Don't do it. A much more effective recourse is to be nice — exceptionally nice. They won't know how to handle it, and eventually will begin giving you the same respect that you give them.

The Demanding Customer

These are the individuals who interrupt you when you are in the middle of a conversation with another customer and demand your immediate attention. Once again, this reaction is borne out of a sense of insecurity. By being demanding, they feel more in control.

Treat them with the same respect you would any other customer, but don't give in to their demands. You can do this by concentrating on their needs and not their manner. Their demands are actually their needs. Think of them as such, and you will be able to respond more positively.

The Indecisive Customer

Like the talkative customer, these individuals can eat up a lot of your time — time you should be spending on other customers. These individuals are truly terrified of making the wrong decision. They don't trust their own judgment. In dealing with indecisive customers, try these approaches:

- **Create a relaxing environment.** If you are calm and understanding, you make them feel more confident and thus better able to make a decision.

- **Limit the possibilities.** This can be done most effectively by finding out ahead of time exactly what it is they want. For example, if you determine they want a black suit to wear for formal occasions, you can limit the number of suits you show them and thus their options.

- **Offer a way out.** Explain the store's return policy. If you say, "You know Mr. Smith, you can return this suit if you decide it's not right for you once you get it home," it will make him less fearful of making a mistake. And chances are, he won't return it. Just knowing he has the option will help him make a decision.

- **Be patient.** If you try to rush these individuals, you're only going to make matters worse. One of their biggest fears is of making a snap decision that they'll regret later. Make it clear that they can take all the time they need. Then, if necessary, you can tell them that while they are thinking about their decision, you will help the next customer.

The Abusive Customer

If a customer becomes abusive, remain calm. Keep reminding yourself that he is not angry at you personally, but frustrated by the situation or other problems in his life.

If the customer begins talking loudly, lower your voice. Doing so will force him to listen more carefully. Eventually, he will lower his voice to match yours.

Talk at a normal pace. If you begin to talk quickly, it will only make matters worse. The customer will think that you are nervous, or worse yet, that you only want to get rid of him.

If a customer uses abusive language or makes threats, be direct. Address the customer by name and say, "Mr. Smith, I understand that you are upset, but do not use that language." If a customer threatens you, document the incident and pass it along to your supervisor.

People With Heavy Accents

Sometimes trying to communicate with foreign-born customers who have heavy accents can be difficult. Misunderstandings can result. To help you deal effectively with individuals who have heavy accents, try these techniques:

- **Be patient and concentrate**. Remember, they are just as frustrated as you are. If you are patient and concentrate on the conversation, you will be better able to understand what they are saying.

- **Speak slowly and distinctly.** Don't speak so slowly that it appears to be an insult, but speak slow enough that they can follow what you are saying. Also, if you speak slowly, they will do the same.

- **Be extra courteous.** This shows them that you really do care and want to help. It also helps them relax and eases their frustration.

- **Avoid using slang or industry jargon.** Use plain, simple English. Don't use terms or phrases that will only add to their confusion.

- **Speak in a normal tone.** Don't shout. When someone is having a hard time understanding us, our first reaction is often to speak louder. Speaking louder won't help; in fact, it will probably only cause more anxiety. And, if you speak louder, the customer will begin to speak louder too.

- **Don't try to listen to every word.** Listen carefully for key words and phrases which sum up what the customer is trying to tell you. If you try to catch every word, you will probably miss the overall message.

- **Reiterate what has been said.** Once the customer has told you what the problem is, summarize what he said, stating your response in the form of a question that can be answered "yes" or "no." For example, "You would like to return this dress because it is the wrong size. Am I correct?"

- **Don't ask, "Do you understand?"** This question sounds negative, and the customer may feel that he is being insulted.

- **Avoid humor or wisecracks.** Stick to solving the problem. Different cultures take humor in different ways. You don't want to risk insulting the customer.

- **Write it down.** If you feel that you are truly not communicating verbally, try writing it down. Many times, foreign-born people can read and write English better than they can speak it. Just like with speaking, use simple, short sentences in expressing your thoughts.

- **If you speak another language, try using it.** The individual you are trying to communicate with may understand the other language better than English.

- **Listen to foreign-language tapes.** If you live in an area where there are a lot of people of a particular foreign nationality, pick up some foreign-language tapes and listen to them. It's not necessary to learn the language, but they will help you become familiar with the foreign sounds.

Handling Complicated Problems

If a customer comes to you with a complicated problem, don't rely on your memory to help get it solved. Listen carefully as the customer describes the problem and take notes.

As is the case with handling any problem, reiterate what the customer has told you to make sure that you fully understand. You can say, "If I understand you, this is what happened." This not only ensures that you understand the situation, it also helps the customer determine if he has left out any relevant facts which will help you solve the problem.

Working With Senior Citizens

Senior citizens have more disposable income today than at any other time. To attract this important segment of the population, many companies are offering special senior citizen incentives. But incentives are not enough to win customer loyalty. Like most people, seniors want to be treated fairly and courteously. Here are some general tips to help you deal with senior citizens.

- **Be cordial.** Take the extra time to be especially warm and friendly. Most seniors appreciate this sort of relationship building.

- **Don't shout.** While you should speak slowly and distinctly, there is no need to shout. If you do, the senior is liable to take it as an insult.

- **Don't patronize.** Chances are the person's IQ is the same as yours. If you talk down to him, you will lose him.

- **Be thorough.** Many seniors keep extensive and exacting records of transactions. They appreciate it if you do the same.

- **Be patient.** At times, you may feel that a senior is being repetitious or long-winded in explaining his problem. Give him the time he needs to explain his situation thoroughly. Reiterating what he told you will convince him that you understood what he said.

- **Be their advocate.** Seniors, like other customers, get frustrated when they feel they are getting the runaround. You can make them your friend if you act as their advocate and help steer them through the company's policies and procedures to find a solution to their problem.

Conclusion

Serving nice people is easy. Difficult people, however, can be a challenge. If you accept this challenge, you will experience great personal satisfaction and, at the same time, win loyal customers for your company.

Customers, no matter how difficult, are people just like you. Sometimes they allow their moods to get in the way. When that happens, remember, don't take it personally. Realizing that other problems are causing their anger should make it easier for you to deal effectively with them.

5

HANDLING COMPLAINTS
AND PROBLEMS

No matter how hard you try, you are bound to eventually have customers who have complaints or problems. How well you handle these situations will determine whether or not the customer remains loyal to your company.

Research has shown that although one in four purchases results in some kind of problem, only 20 percent of customers will actually complain about it. The other 80 percent use problems as an excuse to go elsewhere.

Customers don't complain for three basic reasons:

• They don't believe it will do them any good.

• They don't believe anyone really cares.

• They don't know the proper channels to voice their complaints.

If a customer does complain, accept it as his way of saying he likes you. The customer who complains is giving you the opportunity to correct the problem and make it right. Studies show that people who do complain and have their problems resolved promptly can become a company's most loyal customers.

Of those people who do complain, more than 40 percent are not satisfied with the action taken. Complaints most often involve:

- **Poor service/apathy.** The customer service employee does not live up to the customer's perceived standards for performance or projects an attitude that he just doesn't care.

- **Long waits.** The customer is forced to wait in long lines, put on hold too long on the telephone, or has to wait for the customer service employee who is visiting or doing other things.

- **Rude service people.** The service people that the customer encounters are not helpful and may even be abrasive.

- **Billing problems.** When the customer receives his bill, he discovers that it is not for the amount that the service employee quoted.

- **Unknowledgeable service people.** The service employee does not know enough about the product to resolve the problem properly.

- **Difficulty with returns.** The service employee is uncooperative when the customer attempts to return merchandise.

- **The runaround.** When the customer tries to get help, he is passed from employee to employee without ever getting satisfaction.

- **Unavailability of advertised goods.** The customer goes to the store for the advertised special, only to discover that it isn't available.

Dealing With Customer Complaints

In solving a problem or complaint, remember, you and your customers basically want the same thing: to find a solution. They want to have a positive relationship with your company. If customers didn't care, they wouldn't bother to tell you that there was a problem, they just wouldn't return. When solving customer problems, try these techniques.

- **Listen.** Let the customer explain exactly what the problem is. Don't interrupt, unless it is to clarify a point.

- **Be open.** Don't begin the discussion thinking that the customer is wrong. He may be, but on the other hand, he may not be. Don't say anything that may be interpreted as resistance. Comments like, "Well, I don't know what we can do about that. Let me see," or "I'm not sure if we can help you or not," will only aggravate him. Instead, say something like, "I'm sorry you've experienced this problem. Let me get a little additional information from you so that we can get this matter settled promptly."

- **Identify the problem.** Question the customer about the problem so that you understand exactly what is wrong.

- **Be empathetic.** Let the customer know that you understand how he feels. He will be more at ease and reassured that you can solve his problem.

- **Apologize.** If it is your mistake, say so. Acknowledging the error results in the customer developing trust in you and gives him the confidence that you are willing to solve the problem. A simple "I'm sorry" will go a long way.

- **Ask him what you can do to resolve the problem.** Find out what the customer would like. You may find out that what he wants is actually less than the settlement you are willing to offer.

- **Be prompt.** If you have the authority to make a settlement and what he is asking is fair, don't delay. The quicker you settle the problem, the more likely the customer is to come back. If possible, settle the problem during the initial contact. Prolonging the situation only makes the customer more frustrated which creates additional problems.

- **Keep the customer informed.** If the solution takes a long time, be sure to call and update the customer periodically on the progress.

- **Explain the settlement clearly.** When explaining the settlement, don't leave out any details. Make sure you tell the customer exactly what he can expect.

- **Talk about future transactions.** Let the customer know that the company will try to prevent the same mistake or problem from happening in the future. This demonstrates that your company takes mistakes seriously and wants to correct them. It also tells the customer he is important to your company.

• **Say thank you.** No matter how difficult the transaction, it's a good idea to tell the customer, "Thank you." By thanking the customer, you let him know that you care and that you want to be helpful.

• **Follow up.** Your job is not finished until the customer has received the settlement you promised. Often, this settlement is issued by another employee or department. Be sure to follow through and make sure that everything happens as it is supposed to.

Responding in Writing

Not all complaints are handled face-to-face. Sometimes, a customer will express dissatisfaction in a letter. When this is the case, you have a little longer than usual to formulate your response. But, just like when the customer is standing in front of you, you want to respond appropriately and promptly.

When answering a complaint that has been received in the mail, follow these guidelines:

• **Read the letter carefully.** Don't just skim the letter hoping to find the problem. The only way you can respond appropriately is if you fully understand what the problem is.

• **Write the response in a friendly tone.** Keep your response friendly and positive even when you need to tell a customer you cannot give him what he has requested. Your goal is to keep him as a customer.

• **Keep it simple.** Make sure your response is perfectly clear. Write short, simple, easy-to-understand sentences.

• **Address all problems.** Make sure you answer *all* of the customer's concerns or problems. Although the customer's main complaint may be that he has a defective piece of equipment and wants to return it, he may also be upset about other problems that have occurred. For example, if this is the third product he has tried and they have all been defective, he may want to know why there have been so many problems.

• **Use the customer's name throughout the letter.** By repeating the customer's name you personalize the letter.

- **Make it personal.** It's okay to use a word processor to save on time, but make sure your response does not look like a form letter. Form letters communicate a lack of honest concern and make the customer wonder about the number of complaints you receive. Personalize the letters as much as possible and sign each one individually.

- **Tell him how you plan to resolve the problem.** Let the customer know what steps will be taken to correct the problem and *when*.

- **Talk about future business transactions.** By ending on a positive note and talking about future business transactions with your company, you will increase the chances of him returning.

Following is a sample letter in response to a customer complaint.

Sample Response to Customer Complaint

Dear Mr. Smith:

In response to your letter of August 15, 1989, I am writing to let you know that I have investigated your complaint and discovered the following.

As you stated, our order department did receive your order on June 15. The order was entered into our computer immediately. Unfortunately, shortly thereafter, we experienced a power failure and several orders were lost. Our order people did everything possible to ensure that the lost orders were re-entered, however, yours was inadvertently over-looked.

Mr. Smith, I understand that failing to receive this order on time has caused you to be inconvenienced. Please accept my apology for this error.

As you request in your letter, we have replaced your order. To ensure that it gets to you as soon as possible, we will have it sent to you by overnight delivery service at our expense. I anticipate that it will be delivered to you on August 23. I hope this is satisfactory.

In an effort to prevent this problem from happening in the future, we are initiating a new backup system. All operators will retain a copy of the customer's name and phone number in a special book. In the event of a similar occurrence, we can retrace our steps and ensure that everyone's order is re-entered.

Mr. Smith, we appreciate your business and the opportunity to resolve this problem. We look forward to serving your needs in the future.

If I can ever be of assistance again, please let me know.

Sincerely,

Joe Smith

Dealing With Others to Get Problems Resolved

In order to get a customer's problem resolved, you usually have to work with other people in your company. How you interact with these people will determine how quickly the problem is resolved and how you and the company will look to the customer.

In dealing with others in your company, follow these guidelines:

- **Give the facts.** Tell the individual involved everything that you know about the problem.

- **Explain what solving it means to the customer.** For example, telling someone in your order department that Mr. Smith needs the item ordered immediately for health reasons will probably get the individual to respond a little more quickly than simply saying, "The customer wants it delivered now." If he understands the problem, then he can relate to it better.

- **Don't be accusatory.** Regardless of the situation, don't ever approach another employee and accuse him of causing the problem, or even imply that it is his fault. Remember, your main goal is to satisfy the customer's complaint, and pointing the finger isn't going to help.

- **Suggest a solution.** Be sure to have a potential solution in mind as well as a deadline for completing it. For example, "Since the customer has already made a trip to the store to pick up this item and it wasn't ready, he would like us to ship it to him within the next three days. Is that possible?"

- **Say thank you.** Being courteous to the people you work with is just as important as being courteous to your customers. We all like to be treated with respect. It is also essential if you expect their cooperation in the future.

Eliminating Complaints

Even in the best run companies there are bound to be policies and procedures which can stand improvement. As the front-line person who deals directly with the customer, these problems come to your attention first.

Whenever a customer expresses a comment or complaint about a practice or procedure, write it down and pass it on to your supervisor. Putting it in writing will get results more quickly than simply telling someone. Here's why:

- When you write it down, you can make sure that you have clearly and concisely addressed all aspects of the problem.

- Writing it down puts the complaint and your response on the record. This type of documentation protects you, your company and the customer if there are any further problems with follow-up, product performance or if the customer claims no action was taken.

- Once the problem has been written down, it can easily be routed to all the parties who are involved in correcting it. If you verbalize the complaint and it is passed around, it may become distorted and important details lost by the time it gets to the last person.

- Seeing it in writing will help your supervisor understand the problem more clearly. Stacks of paper are hard to ignore.

When writing the memo, provide the following information:

- The date the complaint was filed and/or the problem occurred.

- A description of what happened.

- The customer's name and phone number (if available).

- A summary of the customer's comments.

- A description of how you handled the situation.

• Your suggestion for correcting the situation.

• Your name and work phone number or extension.

Conclusion

Dealing with complaints does not have to be a negative experience. And if handled properly, they can turn a potentially lost customer into a loyal one.

In dealing with customer complaints, remember that you and the customer have the same goal in mind: to resolve the problem. Keeping this in mind will help you find a solution that is satisfactory to both the customer and your company.

6

KEEPING CUSTOMERS HAPPY

Research shows that businesses spend five times as much to attract a new customer as they do to keep a satisfied customer. Also shown is that each year, 65 percent of a company's business will come from repeat customers.

From these figures, you can see that keeping customers happy is an important part of your job as a customer service employee. But how do you do that?

A good rule to follow is the Golden Rule—"Do Unto Others." Away from your job you are also a customer. Think about the things that you like and dislike about the way service people treat you, and what you learned in Chapter 2 about what customers expect.

Courtesy

Be courteous at all times. Greet the customer with a smile, and if possible use his name. Everyone likes to hear their name. Courtesy pays off in several ways. It:

- **Encourages repeat business.** Customers like to shop where they feel that they are appreciated and where they feel comfortable.

• **Promotes future business.** Word-of-mouth is the most credible and least expensive form of advertising. Customers who are treated courteously will tell their friends about the good experience they had. In fact, according to a recent study, word-of-mouth advertising on a consumer's re-purchase decision is twice as important as corporate advertising.

• **Eliminates interruptions and distractions.** If you are courteous to your customers they will trust you. As a result, you are less likely to have them call to reconfirm a delivery date or double-check their order.

• **Reduces stress.** If you are courteous to your customers, they will be courteous to you. As a result, you will feel good about the job you are doing and be under less stress.

Making the Customer's Experience Easy

Customers like to shop where it's easy. Nobody likes to go into a store and be ignored or deal with a service employee who is not helpful. When a customer walks into a store looking for help and can't find any, chances are he is going to turn around and walk out. For every customer who walks out, the store loses money and you in turn lose a little bit of your job security.

Here are some tips on ways to make a customer's experience with your company easy.

• **Greet the customer warmly.** Walk up to him with a smile and say, "Good Morning," "Good Afternoon," or "Good Evening." Be sure to make eye contact.

• **Shake hands.** Shaking hands is viewed as a friendly, professional gesture.

• **Find out the customer's name.** If you don't know the customer's name, tell him yours. Most people will then, in turn, tell you theirs. If you don't catch the name or you're looking at a document with the customer's name and you're not sure how to pronounce it, be sure to ask. Mispronouncing his name will only annoy him.

• **Don't get distracted.** Give the customer your undivided attention. Don't allow yourself to be distracted by another employee or something else going on around you. Don't try and do two things at once (talk to a customer and fill out a report, for instance).

- **Treat the customer's request as unique.** This may be the hundredth time today someone has requested this specific item from you, but it is the first for the customer. Treat it as such.

Making a customer's experience easy and enjoyable is the best way to keep him coming back. And having him come back costs your company much less than attracting new customers.

When You Make a Mistake

Everyone makes mistakes. But it's the truly mature, professional person who readily admits it. If you make a mistake, you will probably get much further with the customer if you do the following:

- **Accept responsibility.** Even though the customer may be irritated, he will appreciate your honesty. Be direct. Simply say, "I'm sorry your order is not in. It's my fault, I forgot to process it." Your apology may not eliminate the customer's anger and frustration right away, but it will diminish it. Follow your apology with a demonstration of your desire to correct the problem. Say, "I want to do everything I can to correct the problem. What would be a satisfactory solution?"

- **Don't make excuses.** The customer isn't interested in hearing why you made the mistake. His only concern is getting the problem resolved satisfactorily.

- **Negotiate a solution.** Once you've apologized and accepted responsibility, you need to get right on to the business at hand — correcting the mistake. Tell the customer how you intend to correct the problem and see if that's satisfactory. If not, you may have to negotiate.

- **Don't avoid telling the customer.** Tell the customer as soon as you realize you made a mistake. You can turn a problem into an opportunity if you catch the mistake before the customer does and call him to apologize and propose a remedy. While the customer may be unhappy to hear about the problem, he will also appreciate your diligence in catching the mistake and your commitment to correcting it.

When Rules and Regulations Get in the Way

Companies have to have rules and regulations for consistency's sake. But, when taken to extremes, rules and regulations can tie the hands of the customer service employee and make it difficult for him to do his job.

Although rules should not be broken, they should be flexible. Unfortunately, in many companies, customer service employees aren't given the authority to bend rules when necessary.

Review the rules and regulations in your company. Make sure you understand *why* they exist and if there are exceptions to any of the rules. In order to explain them to customers, you need to understand the thinking behind the rules.

Find out if your company allows you to use your discretion when it comes to the rules and exactly how much flexibility you have. Being able to handle a customer's problem, or potential problem, on the spot is sometimes more important than enforcing a rule to the letter.

Take the case of the gentleman who arrived at a hotel at the designated 3 o'clock check-in time only to discover that his room was not ready. Looking irritated he told the desk clerk about how his day had gone. He had missed his first flight and then his second flight had been canceled. Due to all the confusion, he had not eaten lunch.

The desk clerk took the initiative and invited him to go into the hotel's dining room and have lunch at the hotel's expense, even though this was not standard procedure. The man did and by the time he returned, his room was ready and he was in a much better frame of mind.

Stay as flexible as possible while staying within the rules. If you find that a particular rule or procedure causes chronic problems, first document the problems it causes, then talk to your supervisor to see if a change can be made.

Conclusion

Keeping customers happy is imperative if you want them to come back. This can be achieved by displaying common courtesy, making the experience easy and meeting the customer's needs.

As you work with customers, think about how you like to be treated. This will help you provide what others expect.

7

WORKING AS PART OF THE CUSTOMER SERVICE TEAM

As a customer service employee, you are one part of the customer service team. The other two components are your fellow workers and the customer. In order for your transactions with customers to be successful, all three have to work together.

Co-Workers as Part of the Team

Developing good rapport with the people you work with is just as important as developing good relationships with your customers. You need the help of other employees in your company if you are to service your customers effectively.

Everyone in the company works for the customer. They either work directly with the customer, or they work with the people who work with customers. Either way, everyone needs to work together in order to provide the customer with the best possible service.

As a customer service employee, you are on the front line. You are the one who deals with the customer day-in and day-out. Working behind the scenes are many people who support you. If they don't do their jobs, you can't do yours, and if you can't do your job, the company doesn't look good. The philosophy behind teamwork is that everyone works together toward a common goal. If you give co-workers the recognition they deserve, they will be more willing to support you in the future. Following are several suggestions to make sure your "teammates" work *with* you rather than *against* you.

• **Treat them with respect.** The people you work with, like you, appreciate being treated with respect. You aren't happy if someone doesn't appreciate your efforts. The same holds true for your co-workers. Don't be demanding. Even if they are your subordinates, you will get a lot farther if you are polite. Be sensitive to their other responsibilities, deadlines and work load. Don't always insist they drop everything to help you.

• **Develop a relationship.** When possible and it's appropriate, develop a personal relationship as well as a professional one with co-workers. For example, if you know that they are married and have children, you can ask them about their families when you see them in the hall or in the lunchroom. Most people enjoy sharing information about their loved ones. When you show people that you truly care about them as people, they are more likely to want to help you.

• **Make exceptions.** If a co-worker snaps at you or cuts you off, remember that we all have bad days. Don't let his bad day interfere with the job you have to do. Consider this example:

Customer Service Employee:	"Jim, I'm calling about the Bradley order. When will it be finished?"
Jim:	"I don't know. We have so much going on down here there is no way to get it all done."

Instead of demanding that Jim answer your question (which probably won't get you very far) you can use empathy and understanding. An effective response, therefore, might be:

Customer Service Employee:	"I've heard you guys are really overloaded. Is there someone else in your department that has a few minutes who could check this for me? I told the customer I would call him back this afternoon."

With this type of attitude, Jim is more likely to respond favorably to your request, and you get the information you need.

- **Don't lay blame.** Everybody makes mistakes. You don't appreciate being reminded of a mistake that you made, and neither do your co-workers. Stress the positive and avoid the negative. For example, if a co-worker forgot to place an order, don't mention that fact. Just ask, "When do you think we can get it in?"

- **Play by the rules.** Know who you should turn to when there is a problem. Going around a co-worker or over his head isn't going to make you a friend. And when you need that person's help the next time, he is liable to be uncooperative out of spite.

- **Say thank you.** When a fellow employee helps you, say "thank you." It may be part of his job, but everyone likes to feel appreciated. And the next time you are in a bind, that individual will be more likely to help you out — even if it's not part of his job.

- **Praise others.** If a customer thanks you for your efficiency and help, be sure to mention the other people involved. For example, you might say, "If it wasn't for the guys in shipping who called in your order right away we never could have gotten it here on time. They really go out of their way to help our customers." This kind of response makes you and the company look good.

- **Show that you're part of the team.** If a fellow employee comes to you for help, lend a hand whenever you can. If you are willing to help when he needs it, he will be more likely to reciprocate.

- **Give credit.** If a co-worker goes above and beyond the call of duty, let his supervisor know what he has done and how it helped to satisfy the customer's needs. This kind of credit will eventually get back to the employee in the form of praise or maybe even a raise. Once again, if he finds out you were responsible, he will be grateful.

- **Let your co-workers know that they are an important part of the team.** As the person on the front line, you receive immediate feedback from your customers. Your co-workers, however, seldom get this kind of recognition. When a customer expresses pleasure with the way a job was handled and a fellow employee had a part, be sure to let him know. For example you might say, "Jim, you should have seen the expression on Mrs. Jones' face when she stopped in and found her order had arrived in just one day. She was so appreciative that she placed another, even bigger, order. We couldn't have done it without your help. Thanks."

Customers as Part of Your Team

In addition to the people you work with who are part of your team, there is another member you may not even be aware of — the customer. Customers like to be involved in the service process. That's why more and more we are seeing self-service stores and gas stations popping up across the nation.

Contrary to popular belief, the main reason customers pump their own gas, eat in cafeterias and go to self-service grocery stores is not price. Research shows that the main reasons why people choose self-service businesses is because they want to be part of the process, and they feel a sense of accomplishment in doing it themselves.

As a service employee, you can capitalize on this need. When helping your customers, involve them in the process.

- **Ask them for their opinions.** Show your customer several items and ask him for his reaction. For example you may say, "I think the blue one looks nice on you. Which one do you like?"

- **Ask them to tell you about similar products they have used.** For example, if the customer is looking at new stereo equipment, you may ask him questions such as, "What other brands have you purchased? What did you think of their performance?"

- Involve them in the problem-solving process. When there is a problem, ask them what you can do about it to make it right. If they have a say in the matter, then they become part of the solution.

Conclusion

As a customer service employee, you are part of a team. If the company is to be a winner, then the entire team — you, your fellow employees and the customer — have to work together. If you don't, not just one of you will lose, but all of you will.

Like customers, employees want to be treated with courtesy and respect. If you make an effort to build relationships with your fellow employees, you will find that they are willing to help out if you are in a bind.

8

YOUR JOB AS A CUSTOMER SERVICE EMPLOYEE

It takes a certain kind of person to work with the public. As the front-line person in your company, you need to be:

• Familiar with every aspect of the company.

• Outgoing and helpful.

• Able to think on your feet.

• Patient and tolerant.

• Flexible.

• Empathetic.

• A problem solver.

• Cooperative.

• Enthusiastic.

Know Yourself

Your self-image will affect the way you do your job. If you view yourself as a skilled professional, that's probably the image you will project and the way you will act. If, on the other hand, you lack confidence in your skills and abilities, others won't have confidence in you either.

Providing customer service can be a very rewarding experience. When you help someone find what they want or solve a problem, you get immediate feedback in the form of their facial expressions and their comments. But a customer service job can also be trying. For some people, meeting strangers day-in and day-out is no problem — in fact, they find it enjoyable. But for others, the experience can be emotionally draining.

Contact overload is the psychological term used to describe what happens to people who have problems dealing with extensive human contact. Those who suffer from it may experience a number of symptoms including fatigue, apathy, moodiness and, in some cases, hostility toward the people they have to deal with. These reactions can cause problems in an individual's personal life as well as his professional one.

Customer service employees have what has been termed emotionally labor-intensive jobs. In these types of jobs, you must deal with emotions and feelings, both your own and the customer's. Juggling the feelings you bring to work with those you confront on the job is not always easy.

One way to reduce the pressure all these different emotions and feelings generate is to learn to compartmentalize. This means isolating feelings and emotions so you only concentrate on those that are a priority *and* that you can do something about. The others are put aside — compartmentalized — until later when it is appropriate to deal with them.

For instance, say your day started when you discovered the dog chewed up your new pair of shoes. Then you went out to get into your car only to find the battery dead, which caused you to get to work late. Needless to say, by the time you arrive at work, you're not going to be in a very good mood.

As a customer service employee, however, you have to leave all of these negative feelings behind you and concentrate on positive thoughts.

Tell yourself that you will deal with your personal problems when you get home. If necessary, ask your boss if you can have a few moments to collect your thoughts. Take steps to solve the problems that can be dealt with. For example, you may be able to take a few moments to call the local service station and ask them to install a new battery in your car. Put the things you can't do anything about out of your mind. Tell yourself there is nothing you can do about your shoes. Nothing you can do will change the outcome.

First Impressions

Like it or not, people often judge us by the impressions they get in the first few seconds when we meet them. And often, the impression they get lasts a long time.

As a customer service employee who comes in contact with new people hundreds of times a day, judgments are being made of you constantly. If you understand what people react to and how they form these first impressions, you can make a conscious effort to make your first impressions good ones.

Following are some of the outward signs that determine a first impression:

- **Appearance.** How you dress conveys how you see yourself. If your clothes are neat and pressed, the customer perceives you as a detail person. If your clothes are wrinkled and mismatched, he may presume that you are just as sloppy in your work. Clothes can also project an image. If you are dressing appropriately for your business environment, the customer will assume you are a serious professional. Stay away from loud colors and flashy styles. They cause the customer to pay more attention to what you're wearing than what you're saying.

  Grooming is just as important as the clothes you wear. If your hair is greasy, you need a shave, your make-up is too heavy or applied sloppily, or you have body odor, you're not going to make a very good first impression. A good rule of thumb in grooming is to get yourself ready for work each day as if you were meeting someone for the very first time. In your job you are, in fact, meeting a lot of people for the first time.

- **Voice.** The tone of your voice also conveys a lot about you. Take the phrase, "May I help you?" Depending on your tone of voice, it can express several different meanings. If it is said in a friendly, cheerful tone, it conveys that you truly want to help the individual.

If it is said in a gruff, irritated tone, it will give the customer the impression that he has interrupted you, and you don't want to be bothered.

• **Jewelry.** Be conservative in the amount and kind of jewelry that you wear. Flashy jewelry may be acceptable for social occasions, but it will not project the kind of image you want on the job. Also, as in dress, if it's too flashy or if there is too much of it, it will distract the customer from hearing what you have to say.

• **Hair styles.** Conservative is also the approach to take in hair styles. The main objective is to steer away from anything that could prove distracting to the customer. Work is not the place to experiment with extreme styles and unnatural colors.

Good Manners

As children, our parents taught us that good manners were important if we were to get along with others. The same magic words "Please" and "Thank You" that got us a cookie as a child will earn us a loyal customer as an adult.

Whereas good manners will take you a long way in this world, bad manners can hold you back. When you use good manners around your customers, you make them feel comfortable. And, as stated earlier, customers like to shop where they feel comfortable.

In addition to "Please" and "Thank You," there are other good manners which you can practice that will make your customers feel even more comfortable.

• **Avoid informality.** When you first meet someone, don't call him by his first name. By using a title (i.e. Mr., Miss, Mrs., Dr., etc.) you show respect. Continue to address him in that fashion until he indicates he would like you to do otherwise.

• **Avoid discussing controversial issues.** Regardless of what's going on in the world, keep your opinion on any controversial topic to yourself. Religion and politics do not belong in the workplace.

• **Don't tell jokes.** Some people may think of jokes as a good ice breaker, but jokes can backfire. What may not be offensive to you, may be to another person. Therefore, your best bet is to avoid telling jokes.

- **Watch your comments.** Be careful not to make comments that can be misconstrued as being racist, sexist or that may offend any group of people. For example, a phrase like "May I help you dear?" If you are a male employee speaking to a female customer, she may take it as sexist. Or, if you are a female employee speaking to an older lady, she may take it as condescending.

- **Don't smoke around customers.** Although once considered acceptable, smoking is becoming increasingly unpopular among a great many people. Smoke in front of a customer who considers it objectionable and you may lose his business.

- **Don't chew gum or eat around customers.** Gum chewing is annoying to some people. Avoid it altogether. Also, don't bring snacks or your lunch to your customer service area. It not only makes your area look messy, but it can also put off customers. If you're eating when they approach, they may feel like they are interrupting you. Worse yet, in an effort to help them, you may begin talking while you still have food in your mouth.

Develop a Positive Attitude

Your attitude reflects how you think about something or someone. If your attitude is positive, you'll be better able to handle difficult situations. If your attitude is negative, you'll find it hard to handle even the simplest requests.

You determine whether your attitude is positive or negative. In order to develop a positive attitude, try the following:

- Realize that you have control over your attitude.

- Put bad or negative experiences behind you.

- Think about the positive aspects of your job and your life.

- If possible, avoid negative people.

Project a positive image, one that displays pride in yourself, your co-workers and your company.

Dealing With Stress

At one time or another, we all experience stress on the job. But if we learn how to deal with it, stress is less likely to take its toll on us. In order to reduce stress, we must first understand what it is and what causes it. Stress is often the result of uncertainty and anxiety. Often, if we eliminate these factors, we eliminate much of our stress.

Although external factors can play a role in stress, more often than not we bring it on ourselves. Say, for example, you have to call a customer and tell him that you cannot provide the replacement product he requested. He was angry when he brought the broken item back, and you know he is going to blow up again. Instead of handling it first thing in the morning and getting it behind you, you put it off. You make excuses like, "I don't want to call too early in the morning, I may wake him up." At noon you're convinced you can't call because you may interrupt his lunch, and so you put it off again.

The longer you put off calling the customer, the more stress you feel. Don't allow yourself to get into this position. Face problems head-on and you will reduce much of the stress in your life.

Here are some tips on reducing other stressors.

- **Take care of one customer at a time.** Invariably, it seems like everyone comes to you with a question or problem at the same time. Don't allow yourself to get flustered. It won't help you go any faster; in fact, it will probably slow you down. Ask for help when you need it. Don't wait until the situation is totally out of control. If you see that customers are backing up, call your supervisor or a fellow worker and ask for help. If you've established a good working relationship with your fellow employees, this will be easy.

- **If a chronic problem is causing stress, see if it can be changed.** If you are experiencing stress because of a recurring situation, discuss the problem with your supervisor. Allowing it to continue will only cause you unneeded grief and upset customers.

- **Make sure customer complaints are handled.** If they're not, the customer will be calling or coming back and causing you further stress.

- **Reduce stress at home.** Off-the-job stress can filter into your work if you let it. Try to keep things in your personal life on an even keel.

- **Stay informed.** Since a good deal of stress is caused by uncertainty, you need to eliminate it from your life. If you're uncertain about any aspect of your job, ask.

- **Remember to laugh.** When it comes to stress, laughter is the best medicine. Try to find the humor in things, especially stressful situations.

- **Express yourself.** Don't keep emotions bottled up. If you're having a bad day, tell someone you feel you can confide in.

- **Vary your routine.** As the old saying goes, "Variety is the spice of life." It can also help to break up the monotony and thus cut down on your stress.

Managing Your Time

Stress is often caused by the feeling that there is too much to do and not enough time to get it all done. Here are some ways to help you manage your time more effectively.

- **Don't hurry.** When you rush through a task, you often make errors. And correcting errors can take you twice as long as doing the job right the first time.

- **Do the difficult jobs first.** It is human nature to put off difficult tasks for as long as we can. However, your best bet is to do them first thing in the morning when your energy level is at its height. Also, if you put them off until later they are in the back of your mind all day and thus tax your energy for other jobs.

- **Do similar jobs at the same time.** You waste time when you jump from one job to another. It breaks your concentration and thus takes longer. Look at all of the jobs that you have to do and then arrange them in order. For example, if you have to make some telephone calls, answer correspondence and do filing, arrange your day so that you do all of the telephone calling at the same time, the correspondence at the same time and the filing at the same time.

- **Establish goals.** Set goals indicating when you want to have certain tasks completed. When you are successful, reward yourself with a short break or a healthy snack.

- **Maintain a list of simple tasks.** Make a list of tasks that you can do in just a few minutes. Then, when you have a little time between customers, you can start chipping away at them and get these jobs completed.

• **Avoid excuses.** It's easy to say there's not enough time to finish this project tonight, so I'll wait and start tomorrow. But somehow tomorrow never comes, and suddenly you are up against a deadline. Don't procrastinate. Jump in with both feet. Getting started is usually the hardest part of any task.

Conclusion

As the individual who determines how the customer views your company, it's important for you to make sure you display a professional, polished image at all times. Proper dress and grooming, good manners and a positive attitude will help you get a long way.

9

THE CUSTOMER
SERVICE SUPERVISOR

Whether you're currently a supervisor or hope to be one someday, understanding the responsibilities and focus of a customer service supervisor can teach you a great deal about the teamwork concept.

As a supervisor, it's your job to find the best possible people for the job. And once you've found them, you need to keep them motivated.

Some people have negative feelings about service jobs. Some people think of a service employee as the "low man on the totem pole." Others, particularly those whose jobs involve physical labor, see service jobs as "soft" or "easy."

Actually, both couldn't be further from the truth. The customer service employee has one of the most important jobs in the company. It is not an exaggeration to say that how well the customer service employee does his job has a significant impact on the job security of all employees. If a company loses many customers because of poor service, then the future of the entire company is threatened.

Hiring the Right People

Finding the right people to fill these roles can be tricky. You need to find individuals who work well with people, are organized, quick thinkers, empathetic and enthusiastic.

Before you interview for a position, give some thought to the specific skills needed to fill the job. In making your evaluation, do the following:

- **Make a list of the skills the person must possess.** Does the job require any special skills? For example, if they are going to be working with computers, is a knowledge of computers important or do you plan to teach them what they need to know after they have been hired?

- **Determine the specific qualities the individual needs to have.** All customer service employees need to be friendly, outgoing and understanding. But are there other qualities specific to this job that they need? For example, if the job is for a travel agent, maybe you need to find someone who can help customers visualize the perfect vacation?

- **Conduct an informal survey.** Visit with customers in your store to find out what qualities they like to see in service people. What do they feel is important?

The Interview

Develop a job description before you start interviewing. This is your chance to put down in writing exactly what the individual will be expected to do. (More on this topic later in this chapter.)

When you meet with the applicant, your job is to give him as good an idea as possible what the job will entail and your expectations. This is also the time to make a preliminary judgment about how well, or if, he will fit into your organization and how capable he is of doing the job. In the interview consider the following:

- **What is your first impression?** As a customer service employee, customers will judge this individual on the first impression he makes on them. Look at the applicant as the customer would. Is his dress appropriate? Is he well-groomed? Confident?

- **How well does he express himself?** An important part of any customer service job is communication. How freely does the individual communicate with you? Are his responses to your questions well-thought out? Does he have a good command of the language?

- **Is he friendly and outgoing?** As part of the customer service team, he will have to get along with fellow employees as well as the customers. Does he have the necessary people skills to do that?

- **What do his nonverbal clues tell you?** Does he seem calm and relaxed, or is he sitting on the edge of his chair fidgeting? Was his handshake firm, or did it show hesitancy? Does he look you in the eye when he speaks?

- **Does he have ambition?** Is he the type of individual who will be able to move up in the company?

- **Is he bilingual?** If you live in an area where there are a lot of foreign-born residents, knowing a second language could be a plus.

- **Does he have the necessary writing skills?** If he is going to be responsible for answering correspondence, writing memos or putting together reports, make sure that he has good, solid writing skills. Some people are good talkers but have a hard time expressing themselves in writing.

Ask the Right Questions

In addition to your overall impression, you will want to ask questions which indicate how the person will handle various job situations. A good way to do this is to ask him to participate in a role-playing exercise.

Since customer service employees must deal with a lot of different people, some who may even be difficult, use a problem scenario. Play the part of several difficult people, such as the angry customer, the argumentative customer and the non-talker, to see how he responds to each.

Question him about his past work experience. Why did he leave his last job? What did he like most and least about that job? If one of the things he disliked was answering the phone and that will be an important part of this job, he may not be the person you are looking for.

Ask him why he would like to work for your company. This will give you some idea of what he is looking for. Are good company benefits the most important thing to him, or is he looking for a company where he feels there is room for advancement? If he wants to move ahead, find out how long he is willing to wait. He may see this job as a way to get his foot in the door. If he anticipates being promoted in a year and you know there is no possibility for advancement for at least five, you need to let him know up front. Otherwise, he will become dissatisfied, and you will be looking for another employee. Also, find out how he views the role of the customer service employee. Is he sensitive to the importance of meeting a customer's needs? Making the extra effort to build relationships with customers? Building and maintaining good relationships with fellow employees?

A good final question might be how he envisions the job he is applying for. For example, he may view the job as an opportunity to meet fun and interesting people. If the job actually entails sitting behind a desk and taking orders over the phone, he may be sorely disappointed once he gets into the job, and you will be disappointed that he doesn't work out.

In addition to asking the right questions, it's important to listen carefully to his answers. Although you should have a set of prepared questions to ask, don't limit what you ask to what you've prepared. Listen carefully to his responses and then use them as a springboard to further questioning.

Provide the Applicant With a Job Description

Before the applicant ever walks through the door, you need to write a job description. To do this, think about the results you expect. If the position currently exists, talk to those employees who are doing the job to get input on what their job actually entails. If the position does not exist, think carefully about what needs you want to be fulfilled in this position.

The job description should be given to applicants at the interview. It will help you explain the job and demonstrate that you have a clear understanding of the type of person you are looking for.

Here is a sample job description for a customer service representative for a computer store:

JOB TITLE: Customer Service Representative

REPORTS TO: Store Manager

PRIMARY   To work with customers to sell computer
FUNCTION: systems best suited to their needs.

DUTIES AND
RESPONSIBILITIES:

Verbal Communication:	Must possess good speaking and listening skills in order to assess customers' needs.
Writing Skills:	Must be able to compose follow-up letters to customers to reiterate your recommendations.
Telephone Skills:	Must be able to effectively communicate with customers using the telephone.
Attention to Details:	Must be detail-minded. Individual needs to be able to keep accurate records of recommendations made to customers and prices quoted. Must have above average organizational skills which allow the employee to follow-up with customers in a timely manner.
Computer Skills:	Must have basic knowledge of computers and must be willing to take 40 hours of classes to further advance knowledge.

In developing the job description, be sure to list the skills needed in order of importance.

Selecting the Right Employee for the Job

Even though we would like to think that we always choose the best qualified person for the job, it's not always easy to be totally objective. We all have our likes and dislikes, and these have a way of creeping into our subconscious even when we're hiring staff.

The most important thing is to try to find someone who is as closely matched for the job as possible. Even though your decision is bound to be somewhat subjective, it is important to make sure that the person you hire has all of the basic skills and abilities that you need. Don't look at an individual and think, "He'll change," or "We can probably teach him to be more outgoing." There are some skills that can't be taught.

Your Role as Supervisor

As a supervisor, your role is to oversee the work of your subordinates. You need to ensure that they are not only doing their job properly but that they are loyal to the company and remain motivated. Supervision can be tricky, especially if you have no previous experience. As a supervisor, it is your job to delegate work, make sure the job is done right, solve problems and motivate your employees. Instead of taking the time to explain to an employee how to do a job the proper way, you may be tempted to think, "I'll just do it myself." Avoid this line of thinking. Sometimes it *is* easier to do a job yourself, but that's not your function. Your job is to get the most out of the people who work for you. Being a good supervisor means training them to do the job and then making sure that they get it done.

Conclusion

Understanding the role of the customer service supervisor is important if you are going to be an effective member of the team. It's also a good idea to have a true sense of what the job entails in case you have aspirations of moving into management.

In order to hire the right people for the job, it's necessary to do some preparation. If you prepare properly, it will pay off in trusted, loyal employees.

If you get promoted to the position of supervisor through the ranks, take the time to earn the respect of your subordinates. Remember, yesterday they were your fellow employees, so they may take a little time to adjust to the change. Be patient.

10
SUMMARY

As a customer service employee, you have one of the most important jobs in your company. The perception your customers have of your company is due in large part to the way they see you.

In today's service-oriented economy, building strong customer relationships and providing top-notch service are viewed as the only ways companies can survive. You cannot, therefore, take your responsibility lightly.

Your job as a customer service employee is to determine the customer's needs and then meet those needs. What do customers want? Although it's impossible to lump all customers together, there are some basic qualities that customers want when they choose a company to do business with:

- Courtesy.

- Prompt Attention.

- Reliability.

- Empathy.

Generally, the motivating factor *is not* price, it's good service. You may feel that you are providing good service, but that really doesn't matter if your customers don't think so.

The qualities that most customers look for when seeking good service are:

• Personal Attention.

• Responsiveness.

• Dependability.

• Promptness.

• Employee Competence.

• Politeness.

As a service employee, a major part of your job involves communication. Communication is more than a simple dialogue between two people. It involves nonverbal communication, listening and speaking. All are skills you need to develop if you are going to communicate effectively with your customers.

Listening involves more than simply hearing words. You need to listen with your ears and your mind. If you don't fully understand what an individual wants, you can't meet his needs or expectations.

Once you've heard what the individual has said, it's imperative to be sure that you understand it. You can verify this by asking the appropriate questions.

Communicating with a customer by phone is different than communicating in person. You can't rely on body language to help you determine what the customer is thinking.

In communicating by phone there are some basic courtesies that will help to make the transaction more pleasant. These include:

• Answering the phone within three rings.

• Greeting the customer appropriately.

• Speaking in a clear, audible tone.

• Giving the customer your full attention.

• Using the hold button when you need to check on something.

• Never leaving the customer on hold for more than 60 seconds.

In all forms of communication, it is important that you express yourself well. The way in which you say things and the words that you use can say more or less than you anticipated.

Throughout your career you will encounter thousands of different customers. Most will be easy to deal with. But there are some who are difficult to deal with and can cause you problems if you let them.

The important thing in dealing with difficult people is to try to understand what motivates them to behave the way they do. Angry, argumentative and unhappy customers often act the way they do because of external forces. Understanding this will help you deal with them better.

One important thing to remember in dealing with all customers is to keep your emotions in check. Don't allow yourself to get upset regardless of the situation. If you keep a cool head and talk in a calm, rational voice, the individual will begin doing the same thing.

The other thing to remember is to concentrate on what the customer is saying, not how he is saying it. You both have the same goal in mind: to find a solution to the problem.

The important thing in dealing with difficult people is to look at them as a challenge. If you think of them as a problem, it's going to ruin your day. But if you see them as presenting a unique, problem-solving opportunity, you will find your job exciting and rewarding.

Successfully handling complaints is another challenging aspect of your job. As the front-line person in your company, you are the one exposed to most of these.

Think of complaining customers as your friends. The reason they complain is because they like you and they want to help you do a better job. Research tells us that only one in 15 or 20 people complain. Those who don't just go somewhere else.

What customers complain about:

• Poor Service.

• Long Waits.

• Rude Service People.

• Billing Problems.

• Unknowledgeable Service People.

• Difficulty with Returns.

• Getting the Runaround.

• Unavailability of Advertised Goods.

• Problems with Products.

Studies show that prompt attention to a customer's complaint will help win you a loyal customer. And since it costs five times as much to attract a new customer as it does to retain a current customer, it's well worth the effort it takes to try to find an equitable solution.

In dealing with customer complaints, the most important thing is to listen carefully to what the customer is telling you and then respond to each of the concerns that he voices. Don't ignore anything.

Customers also want the customer service employee to show empathy. They want to feel like somebody truly understands how they feel.

Responding to written complaints is a little different than dealing with customers face-to-face. You have longer to formulate a response, but you don't get the immediate feedback that you do when the individual is standing before you.

As in face-to-face communication, you want to ensure that you know exactly what the problem is, keep the exchange friendly and address all of the customer's concerns and problems.

If the same complaints occur again and again, you may want to review your company's policies and procedures to determine if they need to be changed. If so, write a memo to your supervisor explaining the problem and suggest a solution if possible.

In solving customer complaints and problems, it is often necessary to work with others in your company. Developing a good relationship with them ahead of time is an effective tool in accomplishing your goal.

The bottom line in customer relations is to keep the customer happy. How can you do that? The best way is to follow the Golden Rule of "Do Unto Others."

In dealing with customers, think about how you want to be treated. Chances are good that the things you want as a consumer are the same things your customers want.

Customers also want their experience to be as easy as possible. It's your job to make sure that it is.

If you or the company has made a mistake, admit it openly. Don't try to hide it. Doing so only makes matters worse. Accept responsibility for what has happened, discuss possible solutions and get the problem resolved promptly.

As a customer service employee you are part of a very important team. This team consists of you, your co-workers and the customer. All are vital to the success of the company.

Both customers and co-workers want to be treated with respect. If you do so, chances are you will all be winners.

It takes a special person to work with the public. You have to know not only your customer, but also yourself. You must be confident and demonstrate a positive attitude at all times, even when everything seems to go wrong.

Since most of your encounters with customers will be relatively brief, it's important that you project a positive first impression. This is accomplished not only by what you say but also by the way you dress and act.

In dealing with customers, you need to show them your best side all the time. There is no room in customer service for emotional outbursts or rude behavior. Regardless of what has happened outside the job, you need to check your negative thoughts at the door when you come to work.

Providing good customer service benefits you and your company. If customers are happy, they will continue to do business with your company, your company will make a profit and you gain increased job security. If you don't satisfy your customers' needs, they will stop doing business with your company, your company will lose money and your job will be in jeopardy.

When it comes to working with customers, make every effort to go the extra mile. They will notice the effort and, in the long run, you will benefit.

Notes

Notes

LEADERSHIP

Qty.	Item #	Title	U.S. Price	Canadian Price	Total Due
	410	The Supervisor's Handbook, Revised and Expanded	$12.95	$14.95	
	458	Positive Performance Management: *A Guide to "Win-Win" Reviews*	$12.95	$14.95	
	459	Techniques of Successful Delegation	$12.95	$14.95	
	463	Powerful Leadership Skills for Women	$12.95	$14.95	

COMMUNICATION

Qty.	Item #	Title	U.S. Price	Canadian Price	Total Due
	413	Dynamic Communication Skills for Women	$12.95	$14.95	
	460	Techniques to Improve Your Writing Skills	$12.95	$14.95	
	461	Powerful Presentation Skills	$12.95	$14.95	
	482	Techniques of Effective Telephone Communication	$12.95	$14.95	
	485	Personal Negotiating Skills	$12.95	$14.95	
	488	Customer Service: *The Key to Winning Lifetime Customers*	$12.95	$14.95	

PRODUCTIVITY

Qty.	Item #	Title	U.S. Price	Canadian Price	Total Due
	411	Getting Things Done: *An Achiever's Guide to Time Management*	$12.95	$14.95	
	483	Successful Sales Strategies: A Woman's Perspective	$12.95	$14.95	
	489	Doing Business Over the Phone: *Telemarketing for the '90s*	$12.95	$14.95	

LIFESTYLE

Qty.	Item #	Title	U.S. Price	Canadian Price	Total Due
	484	The Stress Management Handbook	$12.95	$14.95	
	486	Parenting: *Ward and June Don't Live Here Anymore*	$12.95	$14.95	
	487	How to Get the Job You Want	$12.95	$14.95	

Subtotal

Special 3-book offer
(U.S. $25.90;
Can. $29.90)

Kansas residents
add 5.5% sales tax

Shipping and handling
($1 one item/.50
each add. item)

TOTAL

Thank you for your Order!

Contents

Let Them Eat Chocolate

Chocolate is mental health food. The wafting aroma of chocolate soothes your senses, whether you're walking into a fresh fudge confectionery or catching the slightest whisper of chocolate cookies baking from next door. Someone should bottle the stuff. *Essence of Chocolate*. Coupled with that sweet scent, chocolate's smooth texture and unsurpassed flavor elicits a comfortable air of well-being, an undeniable aura of content, a veritable state of bliss.

Practically every celebration of peace and happiness brims with chocolate. Try to imagine a birthday, Valentine's Day, Easter morning, Mother's Day, Halloween, or the whole Christmas season *without* chocolate. It simply can't be done. In its own inimitable way, chocolate fosters good will, serenity, and perhaps even sanity on the planet.

In the early 1500s, Spanish explorers learned the use of chocolate from the Aztecs and eventually introduced it to Europe. This not only means that chocolate is American, but also reveals Europe's true motives behind conquering the New World. Introduced to England by 1657 and first manufactured in colonial North America by 1765, chocolate probably played a role in the end of the English Revolution as well as the start of the American Revolution.

Stronger than the worst of days, mightier than the chilliest morning, able to heal bruised egos in a single bite, chocolate, as it were, rules. And

> Ask not what chocolate can do for you, but what you can do for chocolate.

Crazy

ABOUT

Chocolate

COOKBOOK

Credits

Great American Opportunities, Inc.
Favorite Recipes® Press

President:
Thomas F. McDow III
Vice President:
Dave Kempf
Managing Editor:
Mary Cummings
Senior Editors:
Georgia Brazil, Jane Hinshaw, Linda Jones,
Charlene Sproles, Debbie Van Mol, Mary Wilson
Associate Editors:
Lucinda Anderson, Judy Jackson, Carolyn King,
Elizabeth Miller, Judy Van Dyke
Production Designer:
Pam Newsome
Typographers:
Jessie Anglin, Sara Anglin
Essayist:
Robin Crouch
Production:
John Moulton
Manufacturing Assistants:
George McAlister, Karen McClain

This cookbook is a collection of our favorite recipes,
which are not necessarily original recipes.

Published by:
Favorite Recipes® Press, a division of
Great American Opportunities, Inc.
P.O. Box 305142
Nashville, Tennessee 37230

Manufactured in the United States of America
First Printing 1995 38,000 copies

Library of Congress Catalog Number 95-61355
ISBN: 0-87197-808-3

all this power and glory from a seed. Chocolate comes from the seeds of the cacao tree, a pink-flowering perennial, native to South America, which reaches about twenty feet in height, has large waxy leaves, and produces eleven-inch-long seed-pods several times a year. It seems so logical, feels so natural, to know that chocolate does grow on trees. Each yellow or reddish-brown pod is roughly the shape of a giant, elongated nectarine and contains dozens of almond-looking seeds. About two-thirds of the world's output comes from several African countries, while South America provides the remainder.

Cacao seeds are best known as cocoa *beans* and, before processing, they are either purple or off-white in color. The beans are fermented for three to nine days, which turns them brown; then they are dried in the sun, cleaned, roasted, shelled, and ground. During this process, most of the cocoa butter separates from the beans and is used for non-chocolate

> I think that I shall never see a thing as lovely as a cacao tree.

and therefore completely insignificant purposes.

The end result of all this is a rich dark brown, sticky liquid called chocolate liqueur—either used as is to make chocolate candies, syrups, and coatings or filtered and ground into cocoa powder—from which comes all good chocolate things.

Bottom line, cocoa is not only vegetarian, but has a high food value, containing as much as 20 percent protein and 40 percent carbohydrate. Chocolate *is* good food. And—major bonus points—cocoa is mildly stimulating because it contains theobromine, a caffeine-like alkaloid that reportedly stimulates production of the same endorphin released in a state of physical activity. What more does a person need? Chocolate by any other name would be manna.

Available in boundless variety, chocolate is perfect for every occasion and with anything edible. Over fruit, in beverages, topping ice cream, in breads and cakes, as a coating for peanut butter or nuts, in cookies or candies, delicious, nutritious chocolate is something to be crazy about.

Chocolate Walks in Beauty

Chocolate walks in beauty, like the night
Of cloudless climes and starry skies;
And all that's best of dark and light
Meet in its aspect and the sight:
Thus mellowed to that tender bite
Which any other treat denies.

One shade the more, the taste to test,
Had half entranced to nameless grace
Which waves in every morsel best,
Or softly lightens o'er its face;
Where flavors serenely sweet express
How pure, how dear their dwelling-place.

And on that cheek, and o'er that brow,
So soft, so calm, yet eloquent,
The cakes that win, the tortes that glow,
But tell of days in goodness spent,
A mind at peace with all below,
Chocolate, whose love is innocent.

Cakes

Black Forest Cake

2 egg whites	2 egg yolks
1/2 cup sugar	2 ounces unsweetened baking
1³/₄ cups flour	chocolate, melted
1 cup sugar	Cream Center Filling
³/₄ teaspoon baking soda	1 (21-ounce) can cherry pie
1 teaspoon salt	filling
1/3 cup vegetable oil	Chocolate curls
1 cup milk	

Beat egg whites in mixer bowl until soft peaks form. Add 1/2 cup sugar gradually, beating until stiff peaks form. Sift flour, 1 cup sugar, baking soda and salt into bowl. Add oil and half the milk; beat for 1 minute. Add remaining milk, egg yolks and melted chocolate. Beat for 1 minute longer. Fold in egg whites. Spoon into 2 greased and floured 9-inch cake pans. Bake at 350 degrees for 30 to 35 minutes or until layers test done. Cool in pans for 10 minutes. Remove to wire rack to cool completely. Split each layer into halves horizontally. Alternate Cream Center Filling and cherry pie filling between layers of cake. Top with remaining Cream Center Filling and/or pie filling. Garnish with chocolate curls. Yield: 16 servings.

Cream Center Filling

1/4 cup margarine, softened	1/2 cup sugar
1/2 cup shortening	1/2 cup milk
1 teaspoon vanilla extract	2 tablespoons flour

Combine margarine, shortening, vanilla and sugar in mixer bowl; beat for 4 minutes. Blend milk and flour in saucepan. Cook until thickened, stirring constantly. Add to margarine mixture; beat for 4 minutes longer. Yield: 1¹/₂ cups.

Almond Joy Cake

1 (2-layer) package chocolate cake mix
26 large marshmallows
1 cup evaporated milk
1 cup sugar
14 ounces coconut

1/2 cup margarine
1 1/2 cups sugar
1/2 cup evaporated milk
1 cup semisweet chocolate chips
1 cup sliced almonds

Prepare and bake cake mix using package directions for 10x15-inch cake pan. Combine marshmallows, 1 cup evaporated milk and 1 cup sugar in saucepan. Heat until marshmallows melt, stirring to mix well. Stir in coconut. Pour over hot cake. Bring margarine, remaining 1 1/2 cups sugar and 1/2 cup evaporated milk to a boil in saucepan, stirring to mix well. Remove from heat. Stir in chocolate chips until melted. Stir in almonds. Pour over top. Let stand until cool. Yield: 12 to 16 servings.

Candy Bar Round Cake

6 (2-ounce) bars milk chocolate candy
1 cup butter, softened
1 1/2 cups sugar
4 eggs
2 1/2 cups flour
1/4 teaspoon baking soda

1/8 teaspoon salt
1 cup buttermilk
1 cup chopped pecans
1 (5-ounce) can chocolate syrup
2 teaspoons vanilla extract
Confectioners' sugar

Melt candy bars in double boiler. Cream butter and sugar in mixer bowl until light and fluffy. Beat in eggs 1 at a time. Stir in melted candy bars. Mix flour, baking soda and salt together. Add to creamed mixture alternately with buttermilk, beginning and ending with dry ingredients and beating well after each addition. Add pecans, chocolate syrup and vanilla; mix well. Spoon batter into greased 10-inch bundt pan. Bake at 325 degrees for 1 1/4 hours. Cool in pan for 15 minutes. Invert onto cake plate. Garnish with confectioners' sugar. Yield: 16 servings.

Chocolate Applesauce Cake

2 cups applesauce	1½ teaspoons baking soda
½ cup vegetable oil	½ teaspoon salt
2 cups flour	½ teaspoon cinnamon
1½ cups sugar	2 tablespoons sugar
2 eggs	1 cup chopped pecans
2 tablespoons baking cocoa	1 cup chocolate chips

Combine applesauce, oil, flour, 1½ cups sugar, eggs, baking cocoa, baking soda, salt and cinnamon in mixer bowl. Beat at medium speed for 4 minutes. Spoon into greased and floured 9x13-inch cake pan. Sprinkle with mixture of 2 tablespoons sugar, pecans and chocolate chips. Bake at 350 degrees for 40 to 45 minutes or until cake tests done. Yield: 24 servings.

Chocolate and Coconut Cake

1 (2-layer) package devil's food cake mix	2 cups sour cream
3 eggs	1 cup sugar
1 cup water	3 cups coconut
⅓ cup vegetable oil	3 cups whipped topping

Combine cake mix, eggs, water and oil in mixer bowl; mix well. Pour into 2 greased and waxed paper-lined 9-inch round cake pans. Bake at 350 degrees for 35 to 40 minutes or until cake tests done. Cool. Split each layer into 2 layers. Mix sour cream and sugar in bowl. Fold in coconut and whipped topping. Spread between layers and over top and side of cake. Chill, covered, in refrigerator before serving. Yield: 12 servings.

Chocolate Ice Cream Cake

1 (2-layer) package chocolate cake mix 3 eggs	1 pint low-fat chocolate ice cream, softened 1 cup water

Combine cake mix, eggs, ice cream and water in bowl; mix well. Pour into greased bundt pan. Bake at 350 degrees for 45 minutes. Cool in pan for several minutes. Invert onto serving plate. Yield: 16 servings.

Chocolate Malt Ice Cream Cake

1 (2-layer) package dark chocolate cake mix 3/4 cup milk 1/3 cup vegetable oil 3 eggs 2 cups confectioners' sugar 1 (12-ounce) can evaporated milk	1/2 cup butter 1 cup semisweet chocolate chips 1 teaspoon vanilla extract 3/4 cup malted milk powder 1 quart chocolate ice cream Whipped topping Maraschino cherries

Combine cake mix, milk, oil and eggs in mixer bowl; beat at low speed until moistened. Beat at high speed for 2 minutes. Pour batter into 2 greased and floured 9x13-inch cake pans. Bake at 350 degrees for 14 to 17 minutes or until cake tests done; do not overbake. Cool in pans for 15 minutes. Remove 1 cake to wire rack to cool completely. Combine confectioners' sugar, evaporated milk, butter and chocolate chips in heavy saucepan. Bring to a boil over medium heat, stirring occasionally; remove from heat. Stir in vanilla. Let stand for 1 hour; do not stir. Combine malted milk powder and ice cream in bowl; mix well. Spread over cake layer in pan. Top with remaining cake layer. Spread cooled topping over top. Freeze until serving time. Let stand at room temperature for several minutes before cutting into squares. Garnish with whipped topping and maraschino cherries. Yield: 16 to 20 servings.

Chocolate Truffle Cake

16 ounces semisweet baking chocolate
½ cup unsalted butter
1½ teaspoons flour
1½ teaspoons sugar

1 teaspoon hot water
4 egg yolks
4 egg whites, stiffly beaten
1 cup whipping cream

Melt chocolate and butter in double boiler, stirring frequently. Add flour, sugar and water; blend well. Add egg yolks 1 at a time, beating well after each addition. Fold in egg whites gently. Pour into 8-inch springform pan greased on bottom only. Bake at 425 degrees for 15 minutes only. Cake will appear unbaked in center. Cool completely in pan; center will sink slightly. May freeze or store in refrigerator for up to 2 weeks. Spread whipped cream generously over top of cake. Cut chilled cake with warm knife. Let stand at room temperature for 15 minutes before serving. Yield: 8 to 12 servings.

French Chocolate Cake

16 ounces German's sweet chocolate
1 teaspoon water
1 tablespoon sugar

1 tablespoon flour
⅔ cup butter, softened
4 eggs, separated

Melt chocolate with water in double boiler over hot but not boiling water; remove from heat. Add sugar, flour and butter; mix well. Beat egg yolks vigorously. Blend into chocolate mixture gradually. Beat egg whites until stiff peaks form. Fold gently into chocolate mixture. Spoon into 8-inch round cake pan lined with waxed paper. Bake at 425 degrees for 15 minutes only. Cake will be soft but will stiffen when cool to consistency of cheesecake. Cool completely in pan. Yield: 6 to 8 servings.

Chocolate Upside-Down Cake

1 cup chopped pecans
1 cup coconut
1 (2-layer) package German
   chocolate cake mix
½ cup melted margarine

8 ounces cream cheese,
   softened
1 (1-pound) package
   confectioners' sugar

Mix pecans and coconut in buttered 9x13-inch cake pan, spreading evenly. Prepare cake mix using package directions. Spoon into prepared pan. Combine remaining ingredients in mixer bowl; mix until smooth. Drop by spoonfuls over batter; spread evenly. Bake at 350 degrees for 45 to 50 minutes or until cake tests done. Cool on wire rack. Yield: 15 servings.

Heath Bar Cake

1 (2-layer) package German
   chocolate cake mix
½ (14-ounce) can
sweetened condensed milk

½ cup (or more)
   caramel-fudge topping
12 ounces whipped topping
3 Heath candy bars, crushed

Prepare and bake cake using package directions for 9x13-inch cake pan. Make 32 holes in cake with handle of wooden spoon. Pour condensed milk and caramel-fudge topping over cake. Top with whipped topping. Sprinkle crushed candy over topping. Chill until serving time. Yield: 15 servings.

Freeze a frosted cake before wrapping it for storage
in the freezer and the wrap will not stick to the frosting.
Remove the wrapping before thawing the cake.

Heavenly Hash Cake

4 eggs	1 1/2 cups chopped pecans
2 cups sugar	1 (16-ounce) package
1 cup margarine	marshmallows
1 1/2 cups flour	2 cups confectioners' sugar
1/4 cup baking cocoa	1/2 cup evaporated milk
1/2 teaspoon baking powder	1/4 cup melted margarine
2 teaspoons vanilla extract	1/4 cup baking cocoa

Beat eggs, sugar and 1 cup margarine in bowl. Add flour, 1/4 cup baking cocoa, baking powder, vanilla and pecans; mix well. Spoon into greased and floured 9x13-inch cake pan. Bake at 325 degrees for 40 minutes. Cover top of cake with marshmallows. Bake for 3 minutes. Combine confectioners' sugar, evaporated milk, melted margarine and remaining 1/4 cup baking cocoa in bowl; mix well. Spread over marshmallows. Yield: 12 servings.

Le Montmorency

2 cups semisweet chocolate	1/3 cup flour
chips	1/2 cup chopped mandarin
3 tablespoons water	oranges
1/2 cup margarine	6 to 7 tablespoons mandarin
4 eggs	orange juice
3/4 cup sugar	

Grease one 8-inch cake pan. Line with waxed paper; grease and flour waxed paper. Combine 1 cup chocolate chips, water and margarine in saucepan. Heat until chocolate and margarine are melted, stirring until smooth. Combine eggs and sugar in top of double boiler over simmering water. Beat until fluffy and doubled in volume. Add flour; mix well. Add chocolate mixture; beat well. Pour into prepared pan. Bake in preheated 375-degree oven for 25 minutes. Cool in pan for several minutes. Invert onto serving plate. Cool for 10 minutes. Cut 3/4-inch deep section from center of cake, leaving 1 1/2-inch border around side. Crumble into bowl. Add oranges; mash thoroughly. Press gently back into center of cake; level with top of border. Melt remaining 1 cup chocolate chips with 1/4 cup orange juice in saucepan, stirring until smooth. Spoon half the mixture over center of cake. Add remaining orange juice to glaze if necessary; spoon over border of cake. Yield: 12 servings.

Mocha Roulade

6 egg whites	1 teaspoon baking powder
1/2 cup sugar	1 teaspoon vanilla extract
6 egg yolks	1/4 cup sifted confectioners'
1/2 cup sugar	sugar
2 cups finely grated walnuts	Chocolate Kahlúa Cream
2 teaspoons instant coffee	

Line 10x15-inch jelly roll pan with waxed paper extending 4 inches beyond end of pan. Grease waxed paper. Beat egg whites in mixer bowl until soft peaks form. Add 1/2 cup sugar gradually, beating until stiff peaks form. Beat egg yolks with 1/2 cup sugar in large bowl for 5 minutes or until very thick. Add walnuts, instant coffee powder, baking powder and vanilla; beat well. Fold in stiffly beaten egg whites. Spoon into prepared pan, spreading evenly. Bake in preheated 350-degree oven for 25 minutes or until top of cake is golden brown. Cover cake immediately with damp towel. Let cake cool to room temperature. Remove towel; invert cake onto 2 overlapping strips of waxed paper sprinkled with confectioners' sugar. Remove waxed paper from cake; trim edge of cake if needed. Spread 2/3 of the Chocolate Kahlúa Cream over cake. Roll to enclose filling, using waxed paper to help roll. Place on long serving plate. Frost surface with remaining Chocolate Kahlúa Cream. Serve with chocolate sauce if desired. Yield: 12 servings.

Chocolate Kahlúa Cream

2 cups whipping cream	3/4 cups chocolate syrup
1 tablespoon instant coffee	2 tablespoons Kahlúa

Beat whipping cream and instant coffee powder in mixer bowl until blended. Add chocolate syrup and Kahlúa gradually, beating until stiff. Yield: 3 cups.

The chocolate log is the Americanized
version of the French Bûche de Noël or Yule log, a
traditional Christmas cake. It is frequently
garnished with baked meringue mushrooms.

Mocha Torte

1 cup butter, softened
1 1/2 cups confectioners'
  sugar
Pinch of salt
1 teaspoon vanilla extract
2 ounces semisweet baking
  chocolate, melted

2 eggs, separated
6 tablespoons strong coffee
1 angel food cake
1 cup whipping cream,
  whipped
Chocolate sprinkles
Maraschino cherries

Cream first 4 ingredients in mixer bowl until fluffy. Combine chocolate, egg yolks and coffee in small bowl. Add to creamed mixture; mix well. Beat egg whites until stiff peaks form. Fold into creamed mixture. Split cake into 4 layers. Spread chocolate mixture between layers. Frost with whipping cream. Garnish with chocolate sprinkles and maraschino cherries. Yield: 12 servings.

Love and Kisses Chocolate Cake

1/2 cup baking cocoa
1/2 cup boiling water
4 egg whites
1/4 teaspoon cream of tartar
1/4 cup sugar
3/4 cup cake flour
1 cup sugar
3/4 teaspoon baking soda

1/2 teaspoon salt
1/4 cup vegetable oil
4 egg yolks
1 teaspoon vanilla extract
1 1/2 cups low-fat whipped
  topping
Milk chocolate kisses

Dissolve baking cocoa in boiling water. Cool. Beat egg whites with cream of tartar in mixer bowl until frothy. Add 1/4 cup sugar gradually, beating until stiff peaks form. Combine flour, 1 cup sugar, baking soda, salt, oil, egg yolks, vanilla and cooled chocolate in large mixer bowl; beat at low speed until smooth. Fold in 1/4 of the egg whites. Fold in remaining egg whites. Pour into 2 waxed paper-lined greased and floured 9-inch cake pans. Bake at 350 degrees for 18 minutes or until cake tests done. Cool. Fill decorating tube fitted with rosette tip with whipped topping. Spread remaining whipped topping between layers and over top and side of cake. Pipe reserved whipped topping in lattice pattern over top. Garnish with chocolate kisses. Yield: 12 servings.

Chocolate Marshmallow Cake

1³⁄₄ cups flour	1 cup marshmallow creme
1¹⁄₂ cups sugar	1 ounce unsweetened baking
¹⁄₃ cup baking cocoa	chocolate
1 teaspoon baking soda	3 tablespoons milk
¹⁄₂ teaspoon salt	2 tablespoons margarine
1 cup buttermilk	2 cups sifted confectioners'
¹⁄₂ cup vegetable oil	sugar
1¹⁄₂ teaspoons instant coffee	¹⁄₂ teaspoon vanilla extract
³⁄₄ cup water	¹⁄₂ cup chopped pecans

Combine first 5 ingredients in bowl. Stir in buttermilk and oil until smooth. Blend coffee powder and water in glass measure. Microwave on High for 2 minutes or until boiling. Blend into batter. Spoon batter into greased 8x12-inch glass dish. Microwave on Medium for 15 minutes, turning dish twice. Microwave on High for 6 minutes or until cake springs back when touched, rotating dish once. Spoon marshmallow creme evenly over cake; do not spread. Let stand for 5 minutes. Spread marshmallow creme evenly. Combine chocolate, milk and margarine in glass dish. Microwave on Medium for 1¹⁄₂ to 2 minutes, stirring after 1 minute. Beat in confectioners' sugar and vanilla until smooth. Spread over cake. Sprinkle with pecans. Yield: 15 servings.

Easy Red Velvet Cake

1 (2-layer) package yellow	1 cup milk
cake mix	Pinch of salt
Buttermilk	¹⁄₂ cup margarine, softened
1 (1-ounce) bottle of red	¹⁄₂ cup shortening
food coloring	1 cup sugar
2 tablespoons baking cocoa	2 teaspoons vanilla extract
¹⁄₂ cup flour	

Prepare cake mix using package directions, substituting buttermilk for water. Stir food coloring and baking cocoa into batter. Pour into greased and floured 9x13-inch cake pan. Bake using package directions. Cook next 3 ingredients in saucepan until thickened, stirring constantly. Cool. Cream remaining ingredients in mixer bowl until fluffy. Stir into flour mixture. Beat at high speed until of spreading consistency. Spread over cooled cake. Yield: 24 servings.

Ring of Coconut Fudge Cake

¼ cup sugar
1 teaspoon vanilla extract
8 ounces cream cheese, softened
1 egg
½ cup coconut
½ cup miniature chocolate chips
½ cup margarine
2 teaspoons vanilla extract
2 teaspoons vinegar
2 cups water

3 cups flour
2 cups sugar
6 tablespoons baking cocoa
2 teaspoons baking soda
1 teaspoon salt
1 cup confectioners' sugar
2 tablespoons baking cocoa
2 tablespoons melted margarine
2 teaspoons vanilla extract
1 to 3 tablespoons hot water

Combine ¼ cup sugar, 1 teaspoon vanilla, cream cheese and egg in bowl; beat well. Stir in coconut and chocolate chips. Melt ½ cup margarine in large saucepan; remove from heat. Add 2 teaspoons vanilla, vinegar and water; mix well. Mix flour, remaining 2 cups sugar, 6 tablespoons baking cocoa, baking soda and salt in large bowl. Add vinegar mixture; mix well. Pour half the batter into greased and floured 10-inch tube pan. Spoon cream cheese filling over top. Add remaining batter. Bake at 350 degrees for 50 to 60 minutes or until cake tests done. Cool in pan for 15 minutes. Remove to wire rack to cool. Combine confectioners' sugar, remaining 2 tablespoons baking cocoa, 2 tablespoons margarine and 2 teaspoons vanilla in bowl; mix well. Add 1 to 3 tablespoons hot water to make of glaze consistency. Drizzle over cooled cake. Yield: 16 servings.

Avoid white streaks on the side of your
chocolate bundt cake by dusting the greased pan
with baking cocoa instead of flour.

Sinfully Simple Angel Food Cake

1 package angel food cake
        mix
¼ to ½ cup chocolate chips
12 ounces whipped topping

½ cup cherry preserves
¼ to ½ teaspoon almond
    extract

Prepare and bake cake mix using package directions. Cool using package directions. Slice cake horizontally into 3 layers. Place 1 layer on serving plate. Place chocolate chips in microwave-safe bowl. Microwave on High for 1 to 2 minutes or until melted, stirring frequently. Fold in whipped topping. Spread half the mixture on first layer. Repeat with second layer. Place remaining layer on top. Cut into 10 pieces. Combine preserves and flavoring in bowl; mix well. Serve warm or chilled over servings. Yield: 10 servings.

Spaghetti Squash Chocolate Cakes

2 cups cooked spaghetti
        squash
2½ cups flour
¼ cup baking cocoa
½ teaspoon baking powder
1 teaspoon baking soda
½ teaspoon cinnamon
½ teaspoon cloves

½ cup margarine, softened
½ cup vegetable oil
1¾ cups sugar
½ cup egg substitute
1 teaspoon vanilla extract
½ cup buttermilk
1 cup chocolate chips
½ cup chopped walnuts

Purée squash in blender. Sift flour, baking cocoa, baking powder, baking soda, cinnamon and cloves together. Combine margarine, oil and sugar in mixer bowl; mix well. Add egg substitute, vanilla and buttermilk; mix well. Stir in flour mixture. Add squash, chocolate chips and walnuts; mix well. Pour into 2 greased and floured loaf pans. Bake at 325 degrees for 50 minutes or until loaves spring back when lightly touched. May spread with your favorite fudge frosting for a real taste binge. Yield: 16 servings.

Tunnel of Fudge Cake

1½ cups butter, softened | 1 package double Dutch
6 eggs | frosting mix
1½ cups sugar | 2 cups finely chopped walnuts
2 cups flour |

Cream butter and eggs in mixer bowl. Add sugar, flour, frosting mix and walnuts; mix well. Pour into greased bundt pan. Bake at 350 degrees for 65 to 70 minutes or until cake tests done. Cool in pan for 1 hour. Invert onto serving plate. Cool for 1 hour longer. Frost with favorite frosting. Yield: 8 to 10 servings.

Twinkie Cake

1 (2-layer) package devil's | 1 cup sugar
food cake mix | ¾ cup evaporated milk
½ cup margarine, softened | 1 teaspoon vanilla extract
½ cup shortening | 1 can Dutch chocolate frosting

Prepare cake mix using package directions for two 9-inch layers. Cool completely. Split layers horizontally. Cream margarine and shortening in bowl until light and fluffy. Add sugar; beat until very smooth. Add evaporated milk; beat until fluffy. Beat in vanilla. Spread between cake layers. Spread chocolate frosting over top and side of cake. Yield: 12 servings.

To reduce fat, cholesterol and calories
in your favorite cake mix, substitute an equal amount of
applesauce for the oil called for in the mix. For the
average cake mix, you will reduce the calories by half and
the fat by more than three quarters.

White Chocolate Cake

4 ounces white baking
    chocolate, grated
½ cup boiling water
1 cup butter, softened
2 cups sugar
4 egg yolks
2 teaspoons vanilla extract
2½ cups cake flour
1 teaspoon baking soda
½ teaspoon salt
1 cup buttermilk

4 egg whites
3 egg yolks
1½ cups evaporated milk
1½ cups sugar
¾ cup melted butter
6 ounces white baking
    chocolate, grated, melted
½ cup evaporated milk, heated
1 cup chopped pecans
1 (3-ounce) can flaked coconut

Melt 4 ounces white chocolate in boiling water in small bowl; cool. Cream 1 cup butter and 2 cups sugar in mixer bowl until light and fluffy. Beat in 4 egg yolks 1 at a time. Add melted white chocolate and vanilla; mix well. Sift flour, baking soda and salt together. Add to batter alternately with buttermilk, mixing well after each addition. Beat egg whites until stiff peaks form. Fold into batter. Grease and flour three 9-inch cake pans; line bottoms of pans with greased waxed paper. Spoon cake batter into prepared pans. Bake at 300 degrees for 30 minutes or until layers are light brown and test done. Remove to wire rack to cool. Combine 3 egg yolks and 1½ cups evaporated milk in saucepan. Add 1½ cups sugar and ¾ cup butter. Cook over medium heat for 9 to 10 minutes or until thickened, stirring constantly. Add 6 ounces melted white chocolate; mix well. Stir in ½ cup hot evaporated milk. Fold in pecans and coconut. Spread between layers and over top and side of cake. Yield: 16 servings.

For a frosted cake with a nice appearance, brush
loose crumbs from layers and place one layer rounded
side down on plate. Spread with frosting and add
remaining layer rounded side up. Frost side of cake
with up and down motions of spatula
and frost top last, adding swirls as desired.

White Turtle Cake

1 (2-layer) package yellow
cake mix
1 cup water
1 (14-ounce) can sweetened
condensed milk
1 cup vegetable oil

3 eggs
1 (14-ounce) package caramels
1 cup chopped pecans
White Chocolate Frosting
Supreme

Combine cake mix, water, $1/2$ of the sweetened condensed milk, oil and eggs in mixer bowl; beat well. Spread half the batter in greased 9x13-inch cake pan. Bake at 350 degrees for 30 minutes. Combine remaining sweetened condensed milk and caramels in saucepan. Heat until caramels are melted, stirring frequently. Stir in pecans. Pour over hot cake. Spread remaining batter over caramel layer. Bake for 20 minutes longer. Spread White Chocolate Frosting Supreme on warm cake. Yield: 12 servings.

White Chocolate Frosting Supreme

2 ounces white chocolate or
almond bark
$1/2$ cup margarine, softened
$3/4$ cup shortening

$1^1/2$ teaspoons vanilla extract
1 teaspoon butter extract
$2^1/4$ cups confectioners' sugar

Microwave white chocolate until partially melted. Stir until smooth. Cool. Cream margarine and shortening in mixer bowl until light and fluffy. Blend in flavorings and confectioners' sugar. Stir in white chocolate. Beat at high speed for 2 minutes. Yield: 12 servings.

Candy

Chocolate Truffles

2 (8-ounce) bars chocolate almond candy, grated
12 ounces whipped topping

½ (16-ounce) package vanilla wafers

Melt chocolate in double boiler; remove from heat. Stir in whipped topping. Spoon into bowl. Chill until partially set. Process wafers in food processor until fine crumbs. Drop chocolate mixture by spoonfuls into crumbs; shape into balls. Yield: 48 servings.

Chocolate Blocks

4 envelopes unflavored gelatin
½ cup sugar

1½ cups cold water
2 cups semisweet chocolate chips

Combine gelatin and sugar in saucepan. Stir in water. Let stand for 1 minute. Cook over low heat for 5 minutes or until gelatin is completely dissolved, stirring constantly. Add chocolate chips. Cook until chocolate melts, stirring occasionally. Beat with wire whisk until blended. Pour into 8-inch dish. Chill until firm. Cut into 1-inch squares. May add ½ cup chopped nuts and ½ cup marshmallow creme before chilling for rocky road flavor. Yield: 72 servings.

Coconut Mounds

16 ounces coconut
1 (14-ounce) can sweetened condensed milk
1 (1-pound) package confectioners' sugar

1 teaspoon vanilla extract
2 cups semisweet chocolate chips
½ square paraffin

Combine coconut, condensed milk, confectioners' sugar and vanilla in bowl; mix well. Shape into balls; place on tray. Chill for several hours. Melt chocolate chips with paraffin in saucepan, mixing well. Dip balls in chocolate; place on waxed paper. Let stand until firm. Yield: 40 servings.

Chocolate Cream Fudge

3 ounces low-fat cream
cheese, softened
2 cups sifted confectioners'
sugar
2 ounces baking chocolate,
melted

¹/₂ cup chopped pecans
¹/₄ teaspoon vanilla extract
Salt to taste

Beat cream cheese in mixer bowl until smooth. Add confectioners' sugar gradually, beating until fluffy. Add melted chocolate; mix well. Stir in pecans, vanilla and salt. Press into buttered shallow pan. Chill until firm. Cut into squares. Store, tightly wrapped, in refrigerator. Yield: 36 servings.

Cocoa Fudge

²/₃ cup baking cocoa
3 cups sugar
¹/₈ teaspoon salt

1¹/₂ cups milk
¹/₄ cup butter
1 teaspoon vanilla extract

Mix baking cocoa, sugar and salt in heavy 4-quart saucepan. Stir in milk. Bring to a boil, stirring constantly. Cook to 234 to 240 degrees on candy thermometer, soft-ball stage; do not stir. Remove from heat. Add butter and vanilla; do not stir. Let stand at room temperature until 110 degrees. Beat until mixture thickens and loses its luster. Spread immediately in buttered 8x8 or 9x9-inch dish; cool completely. Cut into squares. Yield: 36 servings.

Microwave Double Chocolate Fudge

1 (14-ounce) can sweetened
condensed milk
2 cups semisweet chocolate
chips

1 ounce unsweetened baking
chocolate
1¹/₂ cups chopped pecans
1 teaspoon vanilla extract

Combine condensed milk, chocolate chips and chocolate in 2-quart glass dish. Microwave, uncovered, on High for 3 minutes or until chocolate melts, stirring after 1 minute. Stir in pecans and vanilla. Spread in buttered 8x8-inch pan. Chill until firm. Cut into 1-inch squares. Yield: 64 servings.

Never-Fail Fudge

4½ cups sugar
1 (12-ounce) can
   evaporated milk
1 cup margarine
1 teaspoon vanilla extract
3 cups chocolate chips

Combine first 4 ingredients in saucepan. Cook for 6 minutes, stirring constantly; remove from heat. Stir in chocolate chips until melted. Spoon into buttered dish. Let stand until cool. Cut into squares. Yield: 96 servings.

Rocky Road Fudge

2½ cups sugar
½ cup margarine
⅔ cup evaporated milk
1 (7-ounce) jar
   marshmallow creme
1 teaspoon vanilla extract
2 cups semisweet chocolate
   chips
¾ cup chopped walnuts
2 cups miniature
   marshmallows

Line 9x13-inch pan with greased foil. Bring first 3 ingredients to a boil in saucepan, stirring constantly. Boil over medium heat for 5 minutes, stirring constantly; remove from heat. Add marshmallow creme, vanilla and chocolate chips; stir until smooth. Add walnuts and marshmallows; mix well. Pour into prepared pan. Chill until firm. Yield: 3 pounds.

Stained Glass Fudge

24 ounces white chocolate
1 (14-ounce) can sweetened
   condensed milk
⅛ teaspoon salt
1½ cups chopped mixed
   gumdrops
1½ teaspoons vanilla extract

Melt white chocolate with condensed milk and salt in heavy saucepan, stirring to mix well. Stir in gumdrops and vanilla. Spread in 9x9-inch dish lined with waxed paper. Chill for 2 hours or until firm. Invert onto cutting board; remove waxed paper. Cut into squares. Store at room temperature in airtight container. Yield: 64 servings.

Velveeta Fudge

8 ounces Velveeta cheese | 2 (1-pound) packages
1 cup butter | confectioners' sugar
1¹⁄₂ teaspoons vanilla extract | ¹⁄₂ cup nuts
¹⁄₂ cup baking cocoa |

Combine cheese and butter in large saucepan over low heat. Heat until melted, stirring constantly; remove from heat. Add vanilla and baking cocoa; blend well. Add confectioners' sugar and nuts; mix well. Pour into buttered 9x13-inch pan. Chill until serving time. Cut into squares. Yield: 60 servings.

Fudge-Mallow Raisin Candy

2 cups semisweet chocolate | 3 cups miniature
chips | marshmallows
1 cup chunky peanut butter | ³⁄₄ cup raisins

Melt chocolate chips and peanut butter in saucepan over low heat, stirring constantly until smooth. Fold in marshmallows and raisins. Pour mixture into foil-lined 8x8-inch pan. Chill in refrigerator until firm; cut into small squares. Yield: 24 servings.

Ritz Mint Patties

8 ounces green candy | 24 Ritz crackers
coating wafers | 8 ounces dark baking
Peppermint oil to taste | chocolate

Melt green candy coating wafers in saucepan. Flavor as desired with peppermint oil. Dip crackers in coating. Chill in refrigerator. Melt dark chocolate in saucepan. Dip chilled patties in dark chocolate, coating well. Let stand until firm. Use peppermint oil very sparingly; it has a much stronger flavor than peppermint extract. Yield: 24 servings.

Nut Clusters

1 (7-ounce) jar marshmallow creme
24 ounces milk chocolate kisses
5 cups sugar
1 (12-ounce) can evaporated milk
½ cup butter
6 cups pecan halves

Mix marshmallow creme and chocolate kisses in large bowl; set aside. Combine sugar, evaporated milk and butter in saucepan. Bring to a boil over low heat, stirring constantly. Cook for 8 minutes. Pour over marshmallow and chocolate mixture, stirring until blended. Stir in pecans. Drop by teaspoonfuls onto waxed paper. Let stand until firm. Yield: 144 servings.

Chocolate Peanut Butter Bites

¾ cup packed brown sugar
1 (1-pound) package confectioners' sugar
2 cups crunchy peanut butter
½ cup unsalted butter, softened
2 cups chocolate chips
1 tablespoon unsalted butter

Combine brown sugar, confectioners' sugar, peanut butter and ½ cup butter in bowl; mix well. Pat into ungreased 10x15-inch dish; flatten with rolling pin. Melt chocolate chips and remaining 1 tablespoon butter in double boiler. Spread over peanut butter layer. Cut into squares. Chill for 15 to 20 minutes; remove from pan. Store in refrigerator. Yield: 150 servings.

Toffee Clusters

1 pound almond bark
2 cups chocolate chips
1 (10-ounce) package butter brickle chips

Place almond bark in glass bowl. Microwave for 5 minutes or until almond bark melts, stirring with wooden spoon frequently. Add chocolate chips. Microwave for 1 to 1½ minutes or until melted. Stir in butter brickle chips. Drop by teaspoonfuls onto waxed paper-lined tray. Yield: 40 servings.

Chocolate Peanut Butter Squares

1 (18-ounce) jar chunky
peanut butter
¹/₂ cup melted butter
¹/₂ cup packed brown sugar

2¹/₂ cups confectioners' sugar
1 teaspoon vanilla extract
1 cup milk chocolate chips
¹/₃ cup butter

Combine peanut butter, ¹/₂ cup melted butter, brown sugar, confectioners' sugar and vanilla in bowl; mix well. Press into buttered shallow pan. Melt chocolate chips with ¹/₃ cup butter in saucepan. Spread over peanut butter mixture. Chill until firm. Cut into squares. Yield: 60 servings.

Chocolate Popcorn Balls

1¹/₂ cup sugar
²/₃ cup light corn syrup
²/₃ cup water
3 tablespoons butter

2 ounces baking chocolate,
finely chopped
1 teaspoon vanilla extract
6 quarts popped popcorn

Bring sugar, corn syrup and water to a boil in saucepan, stirring until sugar dissolves. Cook, covered, for 4 minutes. Cook, uncovered, to 300 to 310 degrees on candy thermometer, hard-crack stage. Remove from heat. Stir in butter, chocolate and vanilla. Beat for 1 minute. Pour over popped popcorn in bowl; mix well. Shape into balls with buttered hands. Yield: 24 servings.

Chocolate Popcorn

1¹/₂ cups sugar
2 ounces unsweetened
baking chocolate

¹/₂ cup light corn syrup
1 cup water
4 quarts popped popcorn

Combine sugar, chocolate, corn syrup and water in large saucepan. Cook to 300 to 310 degrees on candy thermometer, hard-crack stage. Pour over popcorn; stir until popcorn is coated. Yield: 4 to 6 servings.

Tiger Butter

1 cup white chocolate candy coating wafers ½ cup peanut butter	1 cup chocolate candy coating wafers

Melt white chocolate wafers in top of double boiler, stirring constantly. Stir in peanut butter. Melt chocolate wafers in top of another double boiler, stirring constantly. Alternate strips of white chocolate-peanut butter mixture with melted chocolate on waxed paper-lined tray. Swirl with a knife. Cool. Break into pieces. Yield: 1¼ pounds.

White Brittle

16 ounces white baking chocolate	1 cup Spanish peanuts 1 cup broken pretzel sticks

Melt white chocolate in saucepan. Stir in peanuts and pretzels. Spread in thin layer on large tray. Chill in freezer until firm. Break into pieces.
Yield: 16 servings.

White Chocolate Candy

32 ounces white baking chocolate 1 cup peanut butter 1 (24-ounce) jar dry-roasted peanuts	3 cups crisp rice cereal 1 (10-ounce) package marshmallows

Melt white chocolate and peanut butter in saucepan, stirring to mix well. Combine with peanuts, cereal and marshmallows in large bowl; mix well. Drop by spoonfuls onto waxed paper. Let stand until firm. Store in airtight container. Yield: 25 servings.

COOKIES

Chocolate Pecan Pie Bars

3 cups flour	1$\frac{1}{2}$ cups light corn syrup
$\frac{1}{2}$ cup sugar	1$\frac{1}{2}$ cups sugar
1 cup margarine, softened	4 eggs, slightly beaten
$\frac{1}{2}$ teaspoon salt	1$\frac{1}{2}$ teaspoons vanilla extract
1 cup semisweet chocolate chips	2$\frac{1}{2}$ cups chopped pecans

Combine flour, $\frac{1}{2}$ cup sugar, margarine and salt in mixer bowl. Beat at medium speed until mixture resembles coarse crumbs. Press into greased 10x15-inch baking pan. Bake at 350 degrees for 20 minutes. Combine chocolate chips and corn syrup in 3-quart saucepan. Cook over low heat until chocolate melts, stirring constantly. Remove from heat. Stir in remaining 1$\frac{1}{2}$ cups sugar, eggs and vanilla. Stir in pecans. Pour over baked layer. Bake at 350 degrees for 30 minutes or until firm around edges and slightly soft in center. Cool; cut into bars. Yield: 48 servings.

Chocolate Toffee Crescent Bars

1 (8-count) can crescent rolls	1 cup margarine
1 cup packed brown sugar	1$\frac{1}{2}$ cups chopped pecans
	1 cup chocolate chips

Separate roll dough into rectangles. Press over bottom of 10x15-inch baking pan; press perforations and edges to seal. Combine brown sugar and margarine in small saucepan. Bring to a boil, stirring constantly. Boil for 1 minute. Pour over dough. Sprinkle with pecans. Bake at 375 degrees for 14 to 18 minutes or until golden brown. Sprinkle with chocolate chips. Let stand for 2 minutes to allow some of the chips to melt; swirl melted and unmelted chocolate over top. Cool. Cut into bars. Yield: 48 servings.

Use a pizza cutter to slice bar cookies.

Heath Bars

30 saltine crackers	½ cup peanut butter
1 cup packed brown sugar	½ cup chocolate chips
1 cup butter	

Line 10x15-inch baking sheet with crackers. Bring brown sugar and butter to a boil in saucepan. Cook for 1 minute, stirring constantly. Pour over crackers. Bake at 350 degrees for 5 minutes. Spread with peanut butter; sprinkle with chips. Return to oven for 1 minute. Spread chocolate over top. Freeze until firm. Break into pieces. Yield: 30 servings.

Nutty Chocolate Caramel Bars

1 (14-ounce) package caramels	⅓ cup evaporated milk
⅓ cup evaporated milk	¾ cup melted margarine
1 (2-layer) package German chocolate cake mix	1½ cups chopped pecans
	1 cup semisweet chocolate chips

Melt caramels in ⅓ cup evaporated milk in saucepan, stirring constantly. Combine cake mix, ⅓ cup evaporated milk, margarine and pecans in bowl; mix well. Spread half the mixture into lightly greased 9x13-inch baking pan. Bake at 350 degrees for 6 minutes. Pour caramel mixture over top. Sprinkle with chocolate chips. Top with teaspoonfuls of remaining cake batter. Bake for 18 minutes. Cool completely in pan. Cut into bars. Yield: 48 servings.

Use frosting to pipe names of guests on
rectangular cookies for place cards.

Marble Squares

8 ounces cream cheese, softened	2 cups flour
$1/3$ cup sugar	2 cups sugar
1 egg	2 eggs
$1/2$ cup margarine	$1/2$ cup sour cream
$3/4$ cup water	1 teaspoon baking soda
$1^1/2$ ounces unsweetened baking chocolate	$1/2$ teaspoon salt
	1 cup semisweet chocolate chips

Blend cream cheese, $1/3$ cup sugar and 1 egg in small bowl; set aside. Combine margarine, water and chocolate in saucepan. Bring to a boil, stirring constantly; remove from heat. Add flour and 2 cups sugar; mix well. Add 2 eggs, sour cream, baking soda and salt; mix well. Pour into greased 10x15-inch cake pan. Spoon cream cheese mixture over batter; cut through batter several times with knife. Sprinkle chocolate chips over top. Bake at 375 degrees for 25 to 30 minutes or until done. Cut into squares. Yield: 24 servings.

Raspberry Chocolate Supremes

1 cup flour	2 tablespoons milk
$1/4$ cup confectioners' sugar	1 cup vanilla chips, melted
$1/2$ cup margarine	2 ounces semisweet baking chocolate, cut into pieces
$1/2$ cup raspberry jam	1 tablespoon shortening
3 ounces cream cheese, softened	

Combine flour and confectioners' sugar in bowl. Cut in margarine until crumbly. Press into ungreased 9x9-inch baking pan. Bake at 375 degrees for 15 to 17 minutes or until light brown. Spread evenly with jam. Beat cream cheese with milk in mixer bowl. Add melted vanilla chips; mix well. Drop by teaspoonfuls over jam; spread evenly to cover. Chill until set. Melt chocolate and shortening in small saucepan over low heat, stirring constantly. Spread over top. Cool. Cut into bars. Store in refrigerator. Yield: 25 servings.

Butterscotch Brownies

¼ cup melted butter or margarine
1 cup packed light brown sugar
1 egg, beaten
½ teaspoon vanilla extract
¾ cup flour

1 teaspoon baking powder
¼ teaspoon salt
½ cup chopped pecans
½ cup semisweet chocolate chips
¼ cup peanut butter
¼ cup flaked coconut

Cream butter and brown sugar in mixer bowl until light and fluffy. Add egg and vanilla; mix well. Add flour, baking powder, salt and pecans, stirring well. Spread into greased 8x8-inch baking pan. Bake at 350 degrees for 30 minutes or until edges come away from sides of pan. Cool on wire rack. Combine chocolate chips, peanut butter and coconut in top of double boiler. Cook until chocolate is melted, stirring constantly. Spread over cooled brownies; cut into bars. Yield: 20 servings.

Cheesecake Brownies

1¼ cups semisweet chocolate chips
¼ cup butter, softened
½ cup sugar
2 eggs
1 teaspoon vanilla extract
½ teaspoon salt
⅔ cup flour
½ cup sugar

8 ounces cream cheese, softened
2 tablespoons butter, softened
2 eggs
2 tablespoons milk
1 tablespoon flour
½ teaspoon almond extract
¾ cup semisweet chocolate chips

Melt 1¼ cups chocolate chips in double boiler over hot water. Cream ¼ cup butter and ½ cup sugar in large bowl until light and fluffy. Add 2 eggs, vanilla and salt; mix well. Add melted chocolate chips and flour; mix well. Spread in foil-lined 9x9-inch baking pan. Combine remaining ½ cup sugar, cream cheese and remaining 2 tablespoons butter in bowl. Beat until light and fluffy. Add remaining 2 eggs, milk, flour and almond extract; mix well. Stir in remaining ¾ cup chocolate chips. Pour over brownie base. Bake at 400 degrees for 40 to 45 minutes or until brownies test done. Cool in pan completely before cutting. Yield: 16 servings.

Hello Dolly Brownies

10 tablespoons margarine	1 cup coconut
1½ cups graham cracker crumbs	1 (14-ounce) can sweetened condensed milk
1 cup chocolate chips	½ cup chopped pecans

Melt margarine in 9x13-inch baking pan. Press graham cracker crumbs into margarine. Add layer of chocolate chips and coconut. Pour sweetened condensed milk over top; sprinkle with pecans. Bake at 350 degrees for 30 minutes. Cut into squares. Yield: 15 servings.

Praline Brownies

1 (22-ounce) package brownie mix	½ cup chopped pecans
½ cup packed brown sugar	2 tablespoons melted margarine

Grease bottom of 9x13-inch baking pan. Prepare brownies using package directions. Spread in prepared pan. Combine brown sugar, pecans and margarine in bowl; mix well. Sprinkle over batter. Bake at 350 degrees for 30 minutes. Cool on wire rack. Cut into squares. Frost with fudge frosting if desired. Yield: 48 servings.

Princess Brownies

1 (22-ounce) package brownie mix	½ cup sugar
8 ounces cream cheese, softened	1 egg
	½ teaspoon vanilla extract

Prepare brownie mix using package directions. Combine cream cheese and sugar in mixer bowl; beat until smooth. Blend in egg and vanilla. Layer half the brownie batter, cream cheese mixture and remaining brownie batter in greased 9x13-inch baking pan. Cut through with knife to marbleize. Bake at 350 degrees for 35 to 40 minutes or until brownies test done. Cool to room temperature. Cut into squares. Yield: 24 servings.

Raspberry Brownies

3 ounces unsweetened
baking chocolate
½ cup shortening
3 eggs
1½ cups sugar
1½ teaspoons vanilla extract
¼ teaspoon salt
1 cup flour
1½ cups chopped walnuts

⅓ cup raspberry jam
1 ounce unsweetened baking
chocolate, melted
2 tablespoons butter
2 tablespoons light corn syrup
1 cup confectioners' sugar
1 tablespoon milk
1 teaspoon vanilla extract

Melt 3 ounces chocolate with shortening in double boiler over warm water; mix well. Cool slightly. Blend eggs, sugar, 1½ teaspoons vanilla and salt in mixer bowl. Stir in chocolate mixture. Add flour; mix well. Fold in walnuts. Spoon into greased 8x8-inch baking pan. Bake at 325 degrees for 40 minutes. Spread jam over hot brownies. Blend 1 ounce melted chocolate with butter and corn syrup in bowl. Add confectioners' sugar, milk and 1 teaspoon vanilla; mix until smooth. Spread over jam. Garnish with additional walnuts dipped in melted chocolate. Yield: 16 servings.

White Chocolate Brownies

1 (21-ounce) package fudge
brownie mix
½ cup water
½ cup oil
1 egg

¾ cup raspberry preserves
6 ounces almond bark
¾ cup butter, softened
¼ cup confectioners' sugar

Combine brownie mix, water, oil and egg in large bowl; beat 50 strokes by hand. Spread in greased 9x13-inch baking pan. Bake at 350 degrees for 33 to 35 minutes or just until set; do not overbake. Cool on wire rack for 10 minutes. Spread with preserves. Cool completely. Melt almond bark in small saucepan over low heat, stirring constantly; remove from heat. Cool for 30 minutes. Cream butter and confectioners' sugar in mixer bowl until fluffy. Beat in cooled almond bark until smooth. Spread carefully over preserves. Cut into bars. Store in refrigerator. Let stand at room temperature for 5 to 10 minutes before serving. May substitute vanilla milk chips or white baking bar for almond bark. Yield: 36 servings.

Chocolate Kiss Cookies

1 cup margarine, softened
$\frac{1}{2}$ cup confectioners' sugar
1 teaspoon vanilla extract
2 cups flour
1 cup finely chopped walnuts

1 (5-ounce) package chocolate kisses
$\frac{1}{2}$ cup (about) confectioners' sugar

Cream margarine, $\frac{1}{2}$ cup confectioners' sugar and vanilla in mixer bowl until light and fluffy. Add flour and walnuts; mix well. Shape dough around chocolate kisses to form a ball. Arrange on ungreased cookie sheet. Bake at 325 degrees for 12 minutes. Roll warm cookies in $\frac{1}{2}$ cup confectioners' sugar to coat. Cool on wire rack. Yield: 24 servings.

Chocolate Potato Chip Cookies

2 cups flour
1 teaspoon baking soda
1 cup margarine, softened
1 cup sugar
1 cup packed brown sugar

2 eggs
1 teaspoon vanilla extract
1 cup chopped pecans
1 cup chocolate chips
2 cups crushed potato chips

Mix flour and baking soda together. Cream margarine in mixer bowl until light. Add sugar and brown sugar gradually, beating until fluffy. Add eggs and vanilla; mix well. Stir in flour mixture until smooth. Fold in pecans, chocolate chips and potato chips. Drop by tablespoonfuls onto ungreased cookie sheet. Bake at 350 degrees for 10 to 12 minutes or until golden brown. Remove to wire rack to cool. May chill dough for 1 hour for thicker cookies. Yield: 108 servings.

Always leave 1 to 2 inches between cookies
dropped on baking sheet to allow room to spread. Thin
dough will spread more than thicker dough.

Chocolate Snowballs

1 cup butter, softened
1/2 cup sugar
1 teaspoon vanilla extract
2 cups sifted flour

1 cup chopped pecans
1 (5-ounce) package chocolate
  kisses
1/2 cup confectioners' sugar

Cream butter, sugar and vanilla in mixer bowl until light and fluffy. Add flour and pecans; mix well. Chill in refrigerator. Shape dough around candy, rolling into balls; place on ungreased cookie sheet. Bake at 375 degrees for 12 minutes or just until set but not brown. Remove to wire rack. Sprinkle with confectioners' sugar. Yield: 24 servings.

Chocolate Sugar Cookies

1/2 cup butter, softened
1/2 cup sugar
1 egg
1/2 teaspoon cream of tartar
1/4 teaspoon baking soda

1/4 teaspoon salt
1/2 teaspoon almond extract
1 to 2 teaspoons baking cocoa
1 1/2 cups flour

Cream butter and sugar in mixer bowl until light and fluffy. Beat in egg. Add cream of tartar, baking soda, salt, almond flavoring, cocoa and flour; mix well. Drop by tablespoonfuls onto microwave-safe pan. Microwave on High for 2 1/2 to 3 1/2 minutes, rotating twice. Cool on wire rack. May bake in regular oven at 350 degrees for 8 to 10 minutes. Yield: 18 servings.

Cool cookies completely in a single layer on a wire
rack before storing. Store soft and chewy
cookies in an airtight container and crisp cookies
in a jar with a loose-fitting lid.

Cocoa Kisses

3 egg whites	1 teaspoon vanilla extract
1/8 teaspoon salt	1/2 cup sugar, sifted
1/2 cup sugar, sifted	3 tablespoons baking cocoa
2 teaspoons water	3/4 cup chopped pecans

Whip egg whites and salt until stiff but not dry. Add 1/2 cup sugar gradually, whipping constantly. Add mixture of water and vanilla alternately with remaining 1/2 cup sugar, whipping constantly. Fold in baking cocoa and pecans gently. Drop by spoonfuls onto cookie sheet coated with nonstick cooking spray and shape into cones. Bake at 250 degrees for 1 to 2 minutes or until drops are firm to the touch but soft inside. Remove to wire rack to cool completely. May pipe through pastry bag into star shapes.
Yield: 40 servings.

Florentine Cookies

2/3 cup butter	1/4 cup milk
2 cups oats	1 teaspoon vanilla extract
1 cup sugar	1/4 teaspoon salt
2/3 cup flour	2 cups milk chocolate chips
1/4 cup corn syrup	

Melt butter in saucepan; remove from heat. Add oats, sugar, flour, corn syrup, milk, vanilla and salt; mix well. Drop by teaspoonfuls 3 inches apart onto foil-lined cookie sheet. Flatten with rubber spatula. Bake at 375 degrees for 5 to 7 minutes or until golden brown. Cool and peel off foil. Melt chocolate chips over hot but not boiling water, stirring until smooth. Spread over smooth side of half the cookies; top with remaining cookies. May remove hot cookies from cookie sheet and place over small inverted custard cups. Let cool and use as dessert shells for ice cream, sautéed apples or other filling.
Yield: 24 servings.

Krispie Chocolate Chip Cookies

1 cup margarine, softened	1 teaspoon salt
2 cups sugar	1 teaspoon baking powder
2 teaspoons vanilla extract	1 teaspoon baking soda
2 eggs	2 cups chocolate chips
2½ cups flour	4 cups crisp rice cereal

Cream margarine and sugar in mixer bowl until light and fluffy. Add vanilla and eggs. Beat for 5 minutes. Sift flour, salt, baking powder and baking soda into mixture; mix well. Stir in chocolate chips and cereal. Drop by teaspoonfuls onto nonstick cookie sheet. Bake at 375 degrees for 9 to 10 minutes or until golden brown. Cool on wire rack. Yield: 60 servings.

Rolo Cookies

1 cup margarine, softened	½ cup chopped pecans
1 cup sugar	1 (9-ounce) package Rolo caramels
1 cup packed light brown sugar	1 tablespoon sugar
2 eggs, beaten	½ cup chopped pecans
2 teaspoons vanilla extract	1 cup vanilla candy coating wafers or chopped almond bark
2½ cups flour	
¾ cup baking cocoa	
1 teaspoon baking soda	

Cream margarine, 1 cup sugar and brown sugar in mixer bowl until light and fluffy. Add eggs and vanilla; mix well. Mix flour, baking cocoa and baking soda together. Stir into creamed mixture. Add ½ cups pecans; mix well. Chill dough for 1 hour. Divide dough into 4 portions; shape each portion into 12 balls. Press 1 unwrapped Rolo caramel into each ball, shaping to enclose completely. Combine remaining 1 tablespoon sugar and remaining ½ cup pecans in small bowl. Dip top of each ball into mixture. Arrange on greased cookie sheet. Bake at 375 degrees for 8 to 10 minutes or until golden brown. Cool on wire rack. Melt vanilla candy wafers in saucepan. Drizzle over cookies. Yield: 48 servings.

Shortbread Chocolate Cookies

1 cup butter, softened
½ cup sugar
2½ cups sifted flour

1 cup miniature semisweet
chocolate chips

Cream butter and sugar in mixer bowl until light and fluffy. Add flour; mix well. Mix in chocolate chips. Divide into 3 portions. Roll each portion into 8-inch circle on cookie sheet; score each circle into 8 wedges. Bake at 325 degrees for 25 minutes or until golden brown. Remove to wire rack to cool. Yield: 24 servings.

Snickers Bar Cookies

1 large package refrigerator
chocolate chip cookies

5 or 6 Snickers candy bars,
sliced ¼ inch thick

Spread cookie dough in 9x11-inch baking pan. Bake using package directions or until almost golden brown. Arrange candy over baked layer. Bake until candy is softened; spread evenly over baked layer. Cool. Cut into squares. Yield: 24 servings.

Toffee Cookies

1 cup butter, softened
1 cup packed brown sugar
1 egg yolk
1 cup flour

6 (1-ounce) bars milk
chocolate candy
⅔ cup finely chopped pecans

Cream butter, brown sugar and egg yolk in bowl until light and fluffy. Add flour gradually, blending well. Spread over bottom of lightly greased 10x15-inch baking pan. Bake at 350 degrees for 15 to 20 minutes or until medium brown. Arrange chocolate candy bars over top of hot baked layer. Let stand until melted. Spread melted chocolate evenly over top; sprinkle with pecans. Cool. Cut into bars. Yield: 75 servings.

Desserts

Buster Bar Dessert

2 cups confectioners' sugar
1½ cups evaporated milk
⅔ cup semisweet chocolate chips
½ cup margarine
1 teaspoon vanilla extract

1 (16-ounce) package Oreo cookies, crushed
½ cup margarine, melted
1 cup Spanish peanuts
½ gallon vanilla ice cream, softened

Combine confectioners' sugar, evaporated milk, chocolate chips, ½ cup margarine and vanilla in saucepan. Cook over medium heat to 280 degrees on candy thermometer, soft-ball stage. Let cool completely. Combine cookies with ½ cup melted margarine in bowl. Press onto bottom of 9x13-inch dish. Cool in refrigerator. Layer peanuts, ice cream and chocolate mixture over prepared crumb crust. Freeze until ice cream is firm. Yield: 20 servings.

Hershey Bar Dessert

1 (8-ounce) Hershey candy bar with almonds
3 (8-ounce) Hershey candy bars without almonds
1¼ cups milk
8 egg yolks, beaten

¼ cup baking cocoa
1 teaspoon vanilla extract
1 (16-ounce) package vanilla wafers, crushed
Whipped cream

Melt candy bars in top of double boiler. Stir in milk. Add a small amount of hot mixture to beaten egg yolks; stir eggs into hot mixture. Blend in baking cocoa. Cook until thickened, stirring frequently. Remove from heat. Add vanilla; mix well. Reserve ¼ cup vanilla wafer crumbs. Alternate layers of remaining vanilla wafer crumbs and chocolate mixture in buttered 8-inch square glass dish, ending with chocolate. Sprinkle with reserved ¼ cup crumbs. Chill in refrigerator for several hours. Let stand at room temperature for 30 minutes before serving. Cut into squares. Garnish with whipped cream. Yield: 9 servings.

Chocolate Dream Crêpes

½ cup semisweet chocolate chips	2 tablespoons water
2 tablespoons margarine	2 tablespoons crème de cacao
½ cup sifted confectioners' sugar	½ teaspoon vanilla extract
	1 quart chocolate ice cream
¼ cup light corn syrup	Chocolate Crêpes
	½ cup chopped pecans

Melt chocolate chips and margarine in double boiler; mix well. Remove from heat. Stir in confectioners' sugar, corn syrup, water, crème de cacao and vanilla. Spoon 3 tablespoons ice cream down center of each crêpe; fold sides over to enclose. Place seam side down on serving plates. Top with warm chocolate sauce; sprinkle with pecans. Yield: 10 servings.

Chocolate Crêpes

½ cup flour	¾ cup milk
1 tablespoon baking cocoa	¼ teaspoon almond extract
2 teaspoons sugar	1 egg
Dash of salt	2 teaspoons melted margarine

Mix flour, baking cocoa, sugar and salt in bowl. Add milk and almond extract; beat until smooth. Beat in egg. Stir in margarine. Chill for 2 hours. Spoon 2 tablespoons batter at a time into hot oiled crêpe pan; tilt pan. Cook for 1 minute or until light brown. Turn crêpe. Cook for 30 seconds. Cool. Stack between layers of waxed paper. Yield: 10 crêpes.

Make a quick and easy sauce for ice
cream or baked pears by melting chocolate-covered
mint patties in the microwave.

Killer Brownie Dessert

2 packages brownie mix
3 large bananas, sliced
2 pints whipping cream, whipped

1 (4-ounce) jar maraschino cherries, drained
4 ounces chopped walnuts

Prepare and bake brownie mix in large baking dish using package directions. Chill for 12 hours. Arrange bananas over brownies. Top with whipped cream; sprinkle with cherries and walnuts. Yield: 12 servings.

Fluffy Lime and Chocolate Dessert

1 (12-ounce) can evaporated milk
1 (3-ounce) package lime gelatin
1 1/2 cups boiling water
2 cups chocolate cookie crumbs

1/2 cup melted butter
1/4 cup lime juice
2 teaspoons lemon juice
1 cup sugar
2 ounces semisweet baking chocolate, shaved

Chill evaporated milk and mixer beaters in freezer for 2 hours. Dissolve gelatin in boiling water in bowl. Chill in refrigerator until partially set. Combine cookie crumbs and butter in bowl; mix well. Spread in 9x13-inch dish. Beat partially congealed gelatin until fluffy. Add lime juice, lemon juice and sugar; mix well. Beat evaporated milk in mixer bowl until fluffy. Fold into gelatin mixture. Spoon into prepared dish. Top with shaved chocolate. Chill for 2 hours or longer. Yield: 12 servings.

Use a vegetable peeler to make chocolate curls.

Chocolate Fromage à la Crème

2 cups flour	1 cup semisweet chocolate
1 cup melted margarine,	chips, melted
slightly cooled	1 teaspoon instant coffee
1 cup chopped walnuts	1½ teaspoons hot water
8 ounces cream cheese,	4 egg yolks
softened	2 tablespoons crème de cacao
½ cup confectioners' sugar	4 egg whites
1 teaspoon vanilla extract	⅛ teaspoon cream of tartar
2 cups whipping cream	½ cup sugar
6 tablespoons	Sliced walnuts
confectioners' sugar	Maraschino cherries

Press mixture of flour, margarine and 1 cup walnuts over bottom of 9x13-inch baking dish. Bake at 350 degrees for 15 minutes or until light brown. Beat cream cheese, ½ cup confectioners' sugar, vanilla and 2 tablespoons whipping cream in bowl until smooth. Whip remaining whipping cream with 6 tablespoons confectioners' sugar in bowl until soft peaks form. Fold ⅔ of the whipped cream into cream cheese mixture. Spread over cooled crust. Chill in refrigerator. Combine chocolate, mixture of instant coffee powder and water, egg yolks and crème de cacao in bowl; beat until smooth. Beat egg whites with cream of tartar, adding sugar gradually and beating until stiff peaks form. Fold into chocolate mixture gradually. Spoon over cream cheese layer in dish. Top with remaining whipped cream. Chill until serving time. Garnish servings with sliced walnuts and cherries. Yield: 8 servings.

Mocha Cream Torte

1 pint whipping cream	2 teaspoons instant coffee
1 cup confectioners' sugar	1 (16-ounce) package graham
3 tablespoons chocolate	crackers
syrup	Shaved chocolate

Whip cream in mixer bowl until soft peaks form. Add confectioners' sugar, chocolate syrup and coffee granules. Layer graham crackers and mocha cream ⅓ at a time in 9x13-inch dish. Chill in refrigerator for 24 to 48 hours. Garnish with shaved chocolate. Yield: 12 servings.

Pastel Mint Refrigerator Dessert

32 Hydrox cookies, crushed	2 cups whipping cream, whipped
1 cup crushed pastel after dinner mints	2 cups miniature marshmallows

Spread half the cookie crumbs in 9x12-inch dish. Combine mints, whipped cream and marshmallows in bowl. Spread over cookie layer; top with remaining cookie crumbs. Chill for 2 days before serving. Yield: 6 servings.

Oreo-Cherry Delight

36 low-fat Oreo cookies, crushed	1 (21-ounce) can light cherry pie filling
1/2 cup margarine, softened	4 cups low-fat whipped topping
1/2 gallon vanilla frozen yogurt	Chocolate syrup
	Chopped pecans

Combine cookie crumbs and margarine in bowl; mix well. Press into 9x13-inch glass dish. Slice frozen yogurt; arrange over crust. Layer pie filling and whipped topping over ice cream. Drizzle with chocolate syrup; sprinkle with pecans. Freeze, covered, until firm. Yield: 8 to 10 servings.

Black Forest Pudding

1 (3-ounce) package cherry gelatin	1 (4-ounce) package chocolate instant pudding mix
1 cup boiling water	2 cups cold milk
1/2 cup cold water	8 ounces whipped topping
1 cup frozen sweet cherries	Grated chocolate

Dissolve cherry gelatin in boiling water in bowl. Add cold water and frozen cherries; mix well. Pour into 6-cup glass serving bowl. Chill until firm. Combine pudding mix with milk in bowl. Prepare using package directions. Pour over congealed layer. Spread whipped topping over pudding. Sprinkle with chocolate. Yield: 4 to 6 servings.

Smashing Mystery Dessert

2 cups packed light brown sugar	1 cup chopped pecans
2 eggs	1 cup miniature chocolate chips
$^2/_3$ cup flour	2 cups whipping cream
1 teaspoon baking soda	1 teaspoon vanilla extract

Combine brown sugar and eggs in mixer bowl; beat well. Add mixture of flour and baking soda; mix well. Stir in pecans and chocolate chips. Spoon into lightly greased 9x13-inch baking dish. Bake at 350 degrees for 25 minutes. Cool for 2 hours. Whip cream in bowl until soft peaks form. Fold in vanilla. Break cake into bite-size pieces. Stir into whipped cream mixture. Spoon into 9x13-inch dish. Freeze for 4 hours to overnight or until firm. Yield: 8 to 10 servings.

Chocolate Peppermint

1 cup crushed chocolate wafers	1 teaspoon vanilla extract
2 tablespoons melted butter	$^1/_2$ teaspoon peppermint extract
$^1/_2$ cup butter, softened	3 eggs
$^3/_4$ cup sugar	$^1/_2$ cup whipping cream, whipped
3 ounces unsweetened baking chocolate, melted	Grated chocolate

Combine chocolate crumbs and 2 tablespoons butter in bowl; mix well. Press lightly into bottom and up side of springform pan. Bake at 350 degrees for 7 minutes. Cool. Cream $^1/_2$ cup butter and sugar in mixer bowl until light and fluffy. Add chocolate, vanilla and peppermint extract; mix well. Add eggs 1 at a time, beating for 3 minutes after each addition. Fold in whipped cream. Spoon into baked crust. Top with grated chocolate. Chill, covered, for 4 hours to overnight. Yield: 10 to 12 servings.

Chocolate Tacos with Fresh Fruit

²/₃ cup sugar	3 cups chopped assorted fresh
½ cup melted margarine	fruit
2 tablespoons water	1 cup whipping cream,
2 eggs	whipped
½ teaspoon vanilla extract	18 ounces semisweet baking
⅓ cup flour	chocolate, broken
⅓ cup baking cocoa	¼ cup margarine
2 tablespoons sugar	¼ cup milk

Grease and flour 3 large baking sheets. Cover spines of two ⅝-inch thick books with foil. Stand books foil side up between 2 books. Combine ²/₃ cup sugar, melted margarine, water, eggs and vanilla in mixer bowl; beat until smooth. Add flour and baking cocoa gradually; beat well. Drop 2 tablespoonfuls batter for each taco onto prepared baking sheet. Spread into 4-inch circle. Bake at 325 degrees for 15 minutes. Remove from baking sheet immediately. Drape 2 tacos over each book, pressing gently to fold. Let stand until cool. Combine 2 tablespoons sugar and fruit in bowl; mix well. Fill each cooled taco with whipped cream and ¼ cup fruit. Combine chocolate, ¼ cup margarine and milk in saucepan. Cook over low heat until chocolate is melted, stirring constantly until smooth. Spoon over filled tacos.
Yield: 10 servings.

Wafer Crush

1 teaspoon instant coffee	½ cup Kahlúa
1 (10-ounce) package	1 cup sour cream
miniature marshmallows	24 chocolate wafers, crushed

Combine instant coffee, marshmallows and Kahlúa in glass bowl. Microwave on High for 2 to 3 minutes or until marshmallows are melted. Stir until smooth. Chill in refrigerator. Stir in sour cream. Alternate layers of chocolate wafer crumbs and sour cream mixture in parfait glasses until all ingredients are used, ending with crumbs. Chill in refrigerator until firm. Yield: 6 servings.

Easy Baked Alaska

1 low-fat yellow loaf cake	4 egg whites, at room temperature
5 (3-ounce) low-fat chocolate-covered ice cream bars	1/4 teaspoon vanilla extract
	1/8 teaspoon salt
	1/2 cup sugar

Cut cake in half horizontally. Place halves cut side up side by side on 10-inch square of foil. Remove sticks from ice cream bars. Arrange ice cream bars on top of cake to within 1/2 inch of edges. Seal with foil. Place in freezer. Beat egg whites with vanilla and salt at medium speed until soft peaks form. Add sugar 1 tablespoon at a time, beating until stiff. Spread over top and sides of cake topped with ice cream bars sealing to edge. Swirl meringue on top in decorative pattern. Place cake on baking sheet. Bake at 500 degrees for 2 to 3 minutes or until golden brown. Remove to cool baking sheet. Freeze for 4 hours or longer. Cut into squares. Yield: 10 servings.

Mocha Ripple Bars

1 1/2 cups chocolate cookie crumbs	1/2 cup whipping cream
1 1/2 teaspoons instant coffee	8 ounces cream cheese, softened
1/2 cup melted margarine	1/2 cup sugar
1 1/4 teaspoons unflavored gelatin	1 1/2 teaspoons vanilla extract
1/2 cup cold water	1 cup whipping cream
1/2 cup sugar	1/4 cup baking cocoa
	1 tablespoon instant coffee

Mix cookie crumbs and 1 1/2 teaspoons instant coffee in bowl. Stir in margarine until well mixed. Press into 7x10-inch dish. Chill in refrigerator. Soften gelatin in water in saucepan. Heat until gelatin dissolves, stirring constantly. Add 1/2 cup sugar and 1/2 cup cream; mix well. Combine cream cheese, remaining 1/2 cup sugar and vanilla in bowl; mix well. Add gelatin mixture; mix well. Whip remaining 1 cup cream until thickened. Fold into cream cheese mixture. Place 1/3 of the mixture in small bowl. Add baking cocoa and remaining 1 tablespoon instant coffee; mix well. Alternate layers of cream cheese mixture and mocha cream mixture onto cookie crumb crust. Stir with knife to marbleize. Chill for 8 hours. Yield: 8 servings.

Boston Cream Cheesecake

1 (9-ounce) package yellow
    cake mix
16 ounces cream cheese,
    softened
1/2 cup sugar
1 teaspoon vanilla extract
2 eggs
1/3 cup sour cream

2 tablespoons cold water
2 ounces unsweetened baking
    chocolate
3 tablespoons margarine
1 cup confectioners' sugar
1 teaspoon vanilla extract
Strawberries

Grease bottom of 9-inch springform pan. Prepare cake mix using package directions. Pour batter into prepared pan. Bake at 350 degrees for 20 minutes. Combine next 3 ingredients in mixer bowl; beat until blended. Add eggs 1 at a time, beating well after each addition. Add sour cream; mix well. Spread over baked layer. Bake for 35 minutes longer. Cool in pan for several minutes. Loosen cake from rim. Cool completely; remove rim of pan. Bring water to a boil in saucepan. Add chocolate and margarine. Cook until melted, stirring frequently. Combine chocolate mixture and confectioners' sugar in mixer bowl; beat well. Add remaining 1 teaspoon vanilla; mix well. Spread over cheesecake. Chill. Top with strawberries. Yield: 10 to 12 servings.

Fudge Truffle Cheesecake

1/2 cup confectioners' sugar
1 1/2 cups vanilla wafer
    crumbs
1/3 cup baking cocoa
1/3 cup melted butter
2 cups semisweet chocolate
    chips

24 ounces cream cheese,
    softened
1 (14-ounce) can sweetened
    condensed milk
4 eggs
2 teaspoons vanilla extract

Combine confectioners' sugar, wafer crumbs, cocoa and butter in bowl; mix well. Press over bottom of 9-inch springform pan. Melt chocolate chips in heavy saucepan over very low heat. Beat cream cheese in mixer bowl until smooth. Add melted chocolate, condensed milk, eggs and vanilla; mix well. Spoon into prepared pan. Bake at 300 degrees for 65 minutes or until center is set. Cool to room temperature. Place on serving plate; remove side of pan. Chill until serving time. Yield: 10 servings.

Lean Chocolate Cookie Cheesecake

1 (9-ounce) package dark chocolate wafers	16 ounces Neufchâtel cheese, cut into chunks
1 egg white, lightly beaten	1/4 cup flour
2 cups nonfat cottage cheese	2 teaspoons vanilla extract
	3/4 cup (or less) sugar
6 egg whites	14 dark chocolate wafers

Pulverize 9 ounces chocolate wafers in blender. Add 1 lightly beaten egg white. Process until moistened evenly. Press over bottom and 1/2 inch up side of 9-inch springform pan. Bake at 300 degrees for 20 minutes. Cool. Purée cottage cheese, remaining 6 egg whites, Neufchâtel cheese, flour, vanilla and sugar in blender. Pour 2/3 of the mixture into prepared pan. Break remaining 14 wafers in half over top, overlapping to cover. Pour remaining cheese mixture over wafer layer, sealing to edge. Place on 10x15-inch baking pan. Bake for 25 minutes or until slightly set. Run knife between cheesecake and side of pan. Cool on wire rack for 30 minutes. Chill, covered, for up to 8 hours. Remove cheesecake; cut into wedges. Yield: 16 servings.

Chocolate Turtle Cheesecake

2 cups crushed vanilla wafers	1 cup chopped pecans, toasted
6 tablespoons melted margarine	1/2 cup sugar
1 (14-ounce) package caramels	16 ounces cream cheese, softened
	1 teaspoon vanilla extract
1 (5-ounce) can evaporated milk	2 eggs
	1/2 cup semisweet chocolate chips, melted

Mix wafer crumbs and margarine in bowl until crumbly. Press over bottom and side of 9-inch springform pan. Bake at 350 degrees for 10 minutes. Melt caramels in evaporated milk in saucepan over low heat until smooth, stirring frequently. Stir in pecans. Pour into prepared pan. Cream sugar, cream cheese and vanilla in mixer bowl at medium speed until light and fluffy. Add eggs 1 at a time, beating well after each addition. Stir in chocolate. Pour over pecans. Bake for 40 minutes or until set. Loosen from side of pan. Cool in pan; remove side. Chill until serving time. Yield: 8 servings.

White Chocolate Cheesecake

1 (6-ounce) package almond toffee bits	32 ounces cream cheese, softened
1 (8-ounce) package chocolate wafers	4 eggs
½ cup blanched toasted almonds	1 egg yolk
2 tablespoons sugar	8 ounces white baking chocolate, melted
1 teaspoon cinnamon	½ cup butter, melted
¼ teaspoon cardamom	3 tablespoons amaretto
6 tablespoons butter, melted	1 tablespoon vanilla extract

Process toffee in food processor container with steel blade until finely ground. Pour into small bowl and set aside. Rinse and dry processor container. Process wafers, almonds, sugar, cinnamon and cardamom in food processor until finely ground. Combine with 6 tablespoons butter in bowl; mix until crumbly. Press over bottom and side of well buttered 10-inch springform pan. Chill in freezer until firm. Beat cream cheese in mixer bowl until light and fluffy. Add eggs and egg yolk 1 at a time, beating well after each addition. Beat in chocolate and ½ cup butter. Add amaretto and vanilla; mix well. Reserve 2 tablespoons ground toffee. Fold remaining toffee into cream cheese mixture gently. Pour into chilled pan. Bake at 300 degrees for 1½ hours or until set in center. Sprinkle reserved toffee over top. Turn off oven. Let cheesecake stand in closed oven for 1 hour. Chill until serving time. Yield: 12 to 15 servings.

Make an easy frozen dessert of torn
angel food cake and softened coffee ice cream. Freeze
mixture in a loaf pan lined with waxed
paper and serve sliced with chocolate sauce.

Heavenly Hash Cake

2 cups chocolate chips	1 cup chopped pecans
4 eggs, separated	1/2 teaspoon salt
2 teaspoons sugar	2 cups whipping cream
1 teaspoon vanilla extract	1 large angel food cake

Melt chocolate chips in saucepan over low heat. Cool. Stir in beaten egg yolks. Beat egg whites until soft peaks form. Add sugar. Beat until stiff peaks form. Fold into chocolate mixture. Add vanilla, pecans and salt; mix gently. Whip cream until soft peaks form. Fold gently into chocolate mixture. Tear cake into bite-size chunks. Place half the cake in bottom of deep bowl or tube pan. Layer half the chocolate mixture, remaining cake and remaining chocolate mixture on top. Chill overnight. Invert onto serving plate. Cut into slices. Yield: 10 to 15 servings.

Mallard's Fondue

2 cups heavy cream	Marshmallows
4 ounces cream cheese	Strawberries
6 to 8 ounces semisweet	Bananas
baking chocolate	Angel food cake
1 or 2 tablespoons Cognac	

Bring cream to a boil in saucepan over medium heat. Add cream cheese. Cook until cream cheese melts, stirring occasionally. Break chocolate into pieces. Add to hot mixture. Cook until chocolate melts, stirring frequently. Stir in Cognac just before serving. Serve with marshmallows, strawberries, bananas and angel food cake squares for dipping. Yield: 3 cups.

Chocolate Fondue

1½ cups semisweet
    chocolate chips
½ cup evaporated skim milk
½ cup light corn syrup
1 tablespoon vanilla extract
1 tablespoon coffee-orange
    liqueur
1 pint strawberries

4 bananas, sliced
1 pineapple, cut into chunks
4 apples, cut into chunks
4 mandarin oranges, cut into
    chunks
4 kiwifruit, cut into chunks
½ pound cake, cut into chunks

Combine chocolate chips, evaporated skim milk and corn syrup in large microwave-safe bowl. Microwave on High for 2½ minutes, stirring twice. Add vanilla and liqueur. Microwave on High for 5 minutes, stirring 3 times. Pour into fondue pot. Serve with fruit and cake. Yield: 12 servings.

Bombe Glacé

3 pints lime sherbet,
    softened
1 pint chocolate or vanilla
    ice cream, softened
2 pints raspberry sherbet,
    softened

1 cup whipping cream
2 tablespoons sugar
Frosted grapes

Spread lime sherbet evenly in 8-cup round mold. Freeze until firm. Spread ice cream evenly over lime sherbet. Freeze until firm. Fill mold to rim with raspberry sherbet. Freeze until firm. Place mold in cold water for several seconds. Loosen edge with knife. Invert onto serving plate. Return to freezer. Whip cream in mixer bowl until soft peaks form. Add sugar; mix well. Spoon into pastry tube. Pipe rosettes around base of bombe. Pipe rosettes in a cross from base to base across top. Pipe rosette cluster on top. Freeze until serving time. Top with frosted grapes if desired. Yield: 16 servings.

Chocolate Ice Cream

5 eggs, beaten
2 cups sugar
1 teaspoon salt
3 cups milk, scalded
5 ounces unsweetened baking chocolate, melted, cooled

2 cups milk
3 cups whipping cream
1 tablespoon vanilla extract

Combine eggs, sugar and salt in double boiler; mix well. Stir in 3 cups scalded milk. Cook over boiling water until thickened, stirring constantly. Add melted chocolate; mix well. Chill in refrigerator. Add 2 cups milk, cream and vanilla. Pour into ice cream freezer container. Freeze using manufacturer's instructions. Yield: 16 servings.

Chocolate and Cherry Ice Cream

1 cup slivered almonds
2 cups sugar
1 cup baking cocoa
6 egg yolks, beaten
6 cups cream

1 teaspoon almond extract
$1/2$ teaspoon vanilla extract
1 cup chopped drained maraschino cherries

Spread almonds in shallow baking pan. Toast at 350 degrees for 8 to 10 minutes or until golden brown, stirring occasionally. Let stand until cool. Chop coarsely and set aside. Mix sugar and baking cocoa in large saucepan. Add egg yolks and 2 cups cream; mix well. Cook over medium heat until very hot, stirring constantly; do not boil. Cool to room temperature. Stir in remaining 4 cups cream and flavorings. Chill for 6 hours or longer. Pour into 5-quart ice cream freezer. Freeze using manufacturer's instructions. Fold in cherries and almonds. Repack freezer cylinder in ice and salt. Let stand for several hours. Yield: 15 servings.

Chunky Chocolate Ice Cream

3 eggs, slightly beaten
1 cup sugar
4 cups milk
2 cups whipping cream
1 (10-ounce) jar
maraschino cherries, drained

1 cup chocolate syrup
3 (1½-ounce) milk chocolate
bars, chopped
1 tablespoon vanilla extract

Combine all ingredients in large bowl; mix well. Pour into 4-quart ice cream freezer container. Freeze using manufacturer's instructions. Yield: 3 quarts.

Chocolate Meringues

2 egg whites
⅛ teaspoon salt
⅛ teaspoon cream of tartar

¾ cup sugar
1 cup chocolate chips
1 teaspoon vanilla extract

Beat egg whites in mixer bowl until foamy. Add salt and cream of tartar. Beat until soft peaks form. Add sugar gradually, beating until stiff peaks form. Fold in chocolate chips and vanilla gently. Drop by small spoonfuls onto greased baking sheet. Bake at 300 degrees for 25 to 30 minutes. Yield: 30 servings.

Easy Chocolate Marshmallow Pizza

1 (24-ounce) roll favorite
refrigerator cookie dough
1 cup peanuts

1 cup marshmallows
1 cup semisweet chocolate
chips

Slice dough; arrange in ungreased 14-inch pizza pan. Press evenly to cover pan. Bake at 375 degrees for 12 minutes. Sprinkle peanuts, marshmallows and chocolate chips on top. Bake for 6 to 8 minutes longer or until marshmallows are golden brown. Yield: 12 servings.

Cocoa Sweetheart Meringues

4 egg whites, at room
temperature
1/2 teaspoon cream of tartar
1 cup sugar
1/4 cup baking cocoa
Sliced fresh strawberries

2 tablespoons butter
1/3 cup baking cocoa
1 cup confectioners' sugar
1/2 cup evaporated skim milk
1/2 teaspoon vanilla extract

Line 2 baking sheets with baking parchment. Draw eight 4-inch hearts 2 inches apart on parchment. Beat egg whites in mixer bowl until foamy. Add cream of tartar. Beat until soft peaks form. Add mixture of 1 cup sugar and 1/4 cup baking cocoa 1 tablespoon at a time, beating at high speed until stiff peaks form. Spoon 1 tablespoon onto each heart; spread to edge. Pipe remaining meringue around edge of hearts using pastry tube fitted with fluted metal tip. Bake at 275 degrees for 1 hour. Turn off oven. Let stand in closed oven until cool. Remove to serving plates. Fill hearts with strawberries. Blend butter and 1/3 cup baking cocoa in saucepan. Stir in confectioners' sugar and evaporated milk. Cook until slightly thickened, stirring frequently. Stir in vanilla. Cool, stirring occasionally. Pour over strawberries. Yield: 8 servings.

White and Black Chocolate Mousse

6 ounces white baking
chocolate
1/2 cup light corn
syrup
2 egg whites
1/4 cup sugar

1/2 cup sifted confectioners'
sugar
2 1/2 cups whipping cream
1/2 teaspoon vanilla extract
8 ounces bittersweet baking
chocolate

Melt white chocolate in saucepan over low heat; remove from heat. Stir in corn syrup. Beat egg whites until soft peaks form. Add sugar gradually, beating until stiff. Fold in white chocolate mixture. Beat confectioners' sugar, 2 cups of the whipping cream and vanilla in bowl until soft peaks form. Fold in white chocolate mixture. Pour into serving bowl. Chill, covered, for 4 to 24 hours. Melt bittersweet chocolate in saucepan over low heat. Cool slightly. Stir in remaining whipping cream. Spoon a small amount of sauce onto serving plates. Top with mousse. Drizzle with remaining sauce.
Yield: 8 servings.

Chocolate Raspberry Mousse

1½ cups macaroon crumbs	4 eggs, at room temperature
½ cup finely chopped toasted almonds	½ cup sugar
6 tablespoons melted butter	12 ounces white baking chocolate, melted
½ teaspoon almond extract	1 cup whipping cream, whipped
1 envelope unflavored gelatin	1 pint raspberries
⅓ cup rum	10 Chocolate Leaves

Mix first 4 ingredients in bowl. Press into 10-inch glass pie plate. Bake at 350 degrees for 7 minutes. Cool. Soften gelatin in rum in double boiler. Heat over simmering water until gelatin dissolves, stirring constantly. Beat eggs in mixer bowl until thick and lemon-colored. Beat in sugar. Add gelatin mixture and chocolate; beat well. Fold in whipped cream. Spoon into prepared pie plate. Chill until firm. Top with raspberries and chocolate leaves. Yield: 10 servings.

Chocolate Leaves

Fresh rose, lemon, camellia, gardenia or ivy leaves	4 ounces sweet or semisweet baking chocolate

Wash rose, lemon, camellia, gardenia or ivy leaves; pat dry. Melt chocolate in double boiler over hot water, stirring constantly. Brush melted chocolate on undersides of leaves with pastry brush. Place on waxed paper or foil-lined tray. Chill for 15 minutes or until firm. Peel leaves carefully from chocolate.

Take advantage of the current popularity of
fancy and flavored coffees and serve them instead of dessert. Add a selection of toppings such as
whipped cream, shaved chocolate, grated orange rind, cinnamon sticks or grated nutmeg.

White Chocolate Mousse

12 ounces white baking chocolate
¾ cup milk
1 envelope unflavored gelatin
¼ cup cold milk
1 teaspoon vanilla extract

4 egg whites, at room temperature
2 cups whipping cream
Dash of lemon juice
1 (10-ounce) package frozen raspberries
1 tablespoon raspberry liqueur

Melt white chocolate in ¾ cup milk in double boiler over hot, but not boiling water; mix well. Remove from heat. Soften gelatin in remaining ¼ cup milk. Add to chocolate mixture; stir until very smooth. Blend in vanilla. Beat egg whites until stiff peaks form. Fold gently ⅓ at a time into chocolate mixture. Whip cream until soft peaks form. Fold with lemon juice into chocolate mixture. Pour into serving bowl. Chill for several hours. Purée raspberries in blender container. Strain to remove seeds. Blend in liqueur. Chill in refrigerator. Spoon sauce over mousse to serve. Yield: 12 servings.

Banana and Berry Brownie Pizza

1 family-size package brownie mix
8 ounces cream cheese, softened
1 egg
1 teaspoon vanilla extract

1 or 2 bananas, cut into ¼-inch slices
1 pint strawberries, sliced
2 ounces semisweet baking chocolate
1 (14-ounce) can sweetened condensed milk

Prepare brownie mix using package directions. Spread batter on greased pizza pan. Bake at 350 degrees for 15 minutes. Combine cream cheese, egg and vanilla in mixer bowl. Beat at medium speed until well blended. Spread over baked brownie crust, leaving ½ inch to 1 inch space around edge. Bake for 15 minutes longer. Cool to room temperature. Arrange bananas and strawberries over baked crust. Combine chocolate and condensed milk in bowl. Microwave until chocolate is melted, stirring occasionally. Microwave for several minutes longer or until thickened, stirring occasionally. Drizzle over fruit. Yield: 8 to 12 servings.

Chocolate Chip Rocky Road Pizza

2¼ cups flour
1 teaspoon baking soda
1 teaspoon salt
1 cup butter, softened
¾ cup sugar
¾ cup packed brown sugar
2 eggs

1 teaspoon vanilla extract
2 cups chocolate chips
1 cup chopped pecans
1 cup chocolate chips
1 cup miniature marshmallows
1 cup chopped pecans

Combine flour, baking soda and salt in bowl. Cream butter, sugar and brown sugar in mixer bowl until light and fluffy. Add eggs and vanilla; mix well. Add flour mixture gradually, beating well after each addition. Stir in 2 cups chocolate chips and 1 cup pecans. Press into 14-inch round pizza pan sprayed with nonstick cooking spray. Bake at 375 degrees for 25 minutes. Sprinkle immediately with remaining 1 cup chocolate chips, marshmallows and 1 cup pecans. Let stand for 5 minutes; swirl topping with knife. Cool to room temperature. Cut into wedges. Yield: 16 servings.

Dirt Pudding

¼ cup margarine, softened
8 ounces cream cheese, softened
1 cup confectioners' sugar
3½ cups milk

2 (4-ounce) packages French vanilla instant pudding mix
16 ounces whipped topping
1 (20-ounce) package Oreo cookies, ground

Cream margarine, cream cheese and confectioners' sugar in mixer bowl until light and fluffy. Combine milk, pudding mix and whipped topping in bowl; mix well. Stir into creamed mixture. Layer cookie crumbs and pudding mixture alternately in a new medium-size flowerpot, ending with cookie crumbs. Insert artificial flowers into top. Yield: 10 to 15 servings.

Mocha-Filled Cream Puffs

¼ cup water	1 egg
2 tablespoons butter	Mocha Cream Filling
¼ cup flour	Confectioners' sugar

Bring water and butter to a full rolling boil in saucepan. Add flour all at once. Cook over low heat for 1 minute or until mixture forms ball, stirring vigorously; remove from heat. Add egg; beat until smooth. Drop by scant ¼ cupfuls onto ungreased baking sheet. Bake at 400 degrees for 35 to 40 minutes or until puffed and golden. Slice small portion from top; scoop out doughy centers. Cool. Fill with Mocha Cream Filling. Dust with confectioners' sugar. Chill until serving time. Yield: 6 to 8 servings.

Mocha Cream Filling

⅔ cup sugar	1½ cups milk
3 tablespoons baking cocoa	1 egg yolk, slightly beaten
3 tablespoons cornstarch	1 tablespoon butter
2 to 3 teaspoons instant coffee	½ teaspoon vanilla extract

Combine sugar, baking cocoa and cornstarch in saucepan. Stir in instant coffee powder and milk. Bring to a boil over medium heat, stirring constantly. Cook for 1 minute, stirring constantly; remove from heat. Stir a small amount of hot mixture into beaten egg yolk; stir egg yolk into hot mixture. Bring just to a boil, stirring constantly; remove from heat. Stir in butter and vanilla. Pour into bowl; cover surface with plastic wrap. Cool. Yield: 6 to 8 servings.

Chocolate Rice

3 cups cooked rice	½ cup sugar
1 tablespoon baking cocoa	1 teaspoon vanilla extract

Place hot rice in serving bowl. Stir in baking cocoa, sugar and vanilla. Serve hot or cold. Yield: 6 servings.

Chocolate Rice Pudding

2 cups rice
2 cups milk
1 teaspoon grated lemon
rind
1 egg yolk
1/4 cup sugar

7 ounces unsweetened baking
chocolate
1 teaspoon butter
1 egg white, stiffly beaten
1/4 cup fine bread crumbs

Cook rice in milk using package directions; strain. Combine lemon rind, egg yolk and sugar in bowl; mix well. Combine chocolate and butter in saucepan. Heat on medium heat until chocolate is melted, stirring occasionally. Remove from heat. Add to egg yolk mixture; mix well. Combine stiffly beaten egg white and rice; mix well. Add to chocolate mixture; mix well. Grease 2-quart baking dish with tube center; sprinkle with bread crumbs. Pour in chocolate mixture. Bake at 350 degrees for 30 to 45 minutes or until set. Cool on wire rack. Invert onto serving plate. May garnish with flavored whipped cream. Yield: 8 servings.

Exquisite Chocolate Sauce

1/4 cup baking cocoa
3/4 cup sugar
1/3 cup light corn syrup
1/3 cup water
1 ounce unsweetened
baking chocolate

3 tablespoons unsalted
butter
1/4 cup whipping cream
1/8 teaspoon salt
1 teaspoon vanilla extract

Sift baking cocoa and sugar together. Cook corn syrup in saucepan until it forms thick threads when dropped from spoon. Stir in water. Add cocoa mixture; mix well. Cook until sugar dissolves, stirring frequently. Add chocolate. Cook until chocolate melts, stirring frequently. Blend in butter and whipping cream. Boil for 15 seconds. Remove from heat. Beat in salt and vanilla. Serve warm or cool. Store in tightly covered jar in refrigerator. Reheat to serve. Yield: 16 servings.

Chocolate Hazelnut Sauce

3 cups whipping cream
1⅓ cups packed brown sugar

14 ounces bittersweet baking chocolate
½ cup butter
½ cup hazelnut liqueur

Combine whipping cream and brown sugar in saucepan; mix well. Add chocolate and butter. Heat until melted. Add hazelnut liqueur. Serve warm over favorite bread pudding. May substitute dark rum, orange liqueur or peppermint schnapps for hazelnut liqueur. Yield: 12 servings.

Hot Fudge Sauce

¼ cup baking cocoa
¼ cup flour
2 cups sugar
1 (12-ounce) can evaporated milk

2 tablespoons butter
1 teaspoon vanilla extract

Combine cocoa, flour and sugar in saucepan. Stir in evaporated milk. Add butter. Bring to a boil, stirring constantly. Cook over low heat for 3 to 5 minutes, stirring constantly; remove from heat. Stir in vanilla.
Yield: 30 servings.

Crispy Chocolate Ice Cream Roll

¼ cup melted margarine
1 (16-ounce) can vanilla frosting

¼ cup light corn syrup
5 cups crisp rice cereal
1 quart chocolate ice cream

Combine margarine, frosting and corn syrup in bowl; mix well. Stir in cereal; coat well. Press into waxed paper-lined 10x15-inch pan. Chill for 30 minutes. Spread ice cream over top. Roll as for jelly roll. Freeze until firm.
Yield: 10 servings.

Mexican Chocolate Sauce

3 ounces unsweetened
baking chocolate
¹/₃ cup butter
4 eggs
1¹/₂ cups sugar

1 cup light corn syrup
1¹/₂ teaspoons vanilla extract
¹/₈ teaspoon cinnamon
1¹/₂ cups pecan halves

Combine chocolate and butter in microwave-safe bowl. Microwave on High until melted. Combine eggs and sugar in mixer bowl; beat well. Add corn syrup, vanilla and cinnamon; mix well. Stir into chocolate mixture. Fold in pecans. Microwave on Medium-High for 5 minutes. Let stand for 5 minutes. Stir well. Microwave on Medium for 4 minutes. Serve warm on ice cream or white cake. Yield: 6 servings.

Butterfinger Angel Food Torte

¹/₄ cup margarine, softened
2 cups confectioners' sugar
4 egg yolks
16 ounces whipped topping
6 Butterfinger candy bars,
crushed

1 (4-ounce) package salted
peanuts, chopped
1 angel food cake, torn into
bite-size pieces

Cream margarine and confectioners' sugar in bowl until light. Add egg yolks; mix well. Fold in whipped topping. Mix crushed candy bars with peanuts in bowl. Layer cake, whipped topping mixture and candy mixture ¹/₂ at a time in 9x13-inch dish. Chill, covered, for 6 hours or longer. Yield: 15 servings.

Be sure to use the correct chocolate for the recipe. Baking
chocolate is available in powder or blocks or liquid
form, but is unsweetened. German's chocolate is used
for baking but has sugar added. Bittersweet,
semisweet and milk chocolate can all be used for cooking
in suitable recipes but in all good candy treats, too.

Chocolate Cinnamon Torte

2 cups sugar
1½ cups butter, softened
2 eggs
2 tablespoons cinnamon
2⅔ cups flour

4 cups whipping cream
¾ cup baking cocoa
3 ounces semisweet baking
   chocolate, grated

Cut out 9 waxed paper circles 9 inches in diameter. Combine sugar, butter, eggs, cinnamon and 2 cups flour in mixer bowl. Beat at low speed until blended. Beat at medium speed until light and fluffy. Stir in remaining ⅔ cup flour. Moisten 2 circles; place on baking sheet. Spread ⅓ cup dough in thin layer on each circle. Bake in preheated 375-degree oven for 8 minutes or until edges are light brown. Cool for 5 minutes. Remove to wire rack to cool completely. Repeat with remaining dough. Peel off paper. Place 1 layer on flat serving plate. Whip cream and baking cocoa in mixer bowl until soft peaks form. Spread ½ cup over layer. Repeat with remaining layers and cream, ending with cream. Top with grated chocolate. Chill for 3 hours or longer. Cut into thin slices. Yield: 16 servings.

Chocolate Malt Ice Cream Torte

1 cup finely crushed
   graham cracker crumbs
3 tablespoons sugar
1 teaspoon cinnamon
3 tablespoons melted
   margarine, cooled
2 tablespoons finely grated
semisweet baking chocolate

½ gallon vanilla or marble
   fudge ice cream
½ cup malted milk powder
4 ounces chocolate-covered
   malted milk balls, coarsely
   chopped

Combine graham cracker crumbs, sugar and cinnamon in bowl; mix well. Stir in margarine and chocolate until well mixed. Press onto bottom and halfway up side of greased springform pan. Let ice cream stand in bowl until soft but not melted. Add malted milk powder; beat until well mixed. Spread over crumb mixture. Sprinkle with chopped malted milk balls, patting lightly into ice cream. Freeze, covered, for 4 hours or until firm. Loosen from side of pan with knife dipped in hot water. Remove pan ring. Cut into wedges. Yield: 10 to 12 servings.

Chocolate Mousse Torte

2 cups chocolate wafer
    crumbs
½ cup melted unsalted
    butter
1 cup whipping cream

12 ounces semisweet baking
    chocolate
3 egg yolks
3 tablespoons orange liqueur

Combine crumbs and butter in bowl; mix well. Press onto bottom and side of greased 10-inch springform pan. Chill for 1 hour. Scald whipping cream in saucepan. Combine chocolate, egg yolks and liqueur in blender container. Process at medium speed while gradually adding hot whipping cream. Blend until smooth. Pour into prepared crust. Chill overnight. Yield: 12 servings.

Fantastic Chocolate Trifle

1 (6-ounce) package
chocolate instant pudding or
    mousse mix
1 (1-pound) chocolate cake,
    cut into small pieces
1 cup Kahlúa or coffee
    liqueur

1 (12-ounce) package brickle
    or crushed English toffee
2 cups whipping cream,
    whipped
1 (7-ounce) package slivered
    almonds
Maraschino cherries

Prepare pudding using package directions. Layer cake, Kahlúa, brickle, pudding and whipped cream ½ at a time in trifle dish or transparent glass bowl. Top with almonds and cherries. Yield: 10 to 12 servings.

Pies

Baked Alaska Pie

2 egg whites
1/4 cup sugar
1 pint to 1 quart favorite
flavor frozen yogurt

1 baked (9-inch) pie
shell

Beat egg whites in mixer bowl until soft peaks form. Add sugar gradually, beating until stiff. Spoon frozen yogurt into pie shell. Spread with meringue, sealing to edges. Bake at 475 degrees for 5 minutes. Yield: 6 to 8 servings.

Black Bottom Pie

14 gingersnap cookies,
finely crushed
5 tablespoons melted
margarine
1/2 cup sugar
1 1/2 tablespoons cornstarch
4 egg yolks, well beaten
2 cups milk, scalded
1 1/2 ounces unsweetened
baking chocolate
1 teaspoon vanilla extract

1 tablespoon unflavored
gelatin
2 tablespoons cold water
4 egg whites
1/2 cup sugar
1/4 teaspoon cream of tartar
2 tablespoons bourbon
1 cup whipping cream
1 tablespoon confectioners'
sugar

Mix gingersnap crumbs and melted margarine in small bowl. Press onto bottom and side of 10-inch pie plate. Bake at 375 degrees for 10 minutes; cool. Combine sugar and cornstarch in top of double boiler. Stir in egg yolks. Add scalded milk; mix well. Stir over boiling water until mixture thickens and coats spoon. Remove from heat. Pour 1 cup custard into small bowl. Add baking chocolate, stirring until melted. Beat well as the mixture cools. Stir in vanilla. Pour chocolate mixture onto bottom of cooled pie crust. Soften gelatin in cold water in large bowl. Pour remaining custard gradually into gelatin, stirring constantly; cool. Beat egg whites at high speed in mixer bowl until soft peaks form. Add remaining 1/2 cup sugar, cream of tartar and bourbon, beating well after each addition until stiff peaks form. Fold into custard mixture gently. Spoon over chocolate mixture in crust. Chill in refrigerator until firm. Whip cream in bowl until soft peaks form. Add sugar, beating constantly. Spread over pie before serving. Yield: 10 servings.

Candy Bar Pie

1⅓ cups coconut
2 tablespoons margarine, melted
1 teaspoon instant coffee

2 tablespoons water
5 (1½-ounce) bars chocolate candy with almonds
4 cups whipped topping

Combine coconut and margarine in bowl; mix well. Press over bottom and side of 9-inch pie plate. Bake at 325 degrees for 10 minutes or until coconut is golden. Cool. Dissolve instant coffee powder in water in saucepan over low heat. Melt candy bars in coffee mixture, stirring constantly. Cool slightly. Fold in whipped topping. Pour chocolate mixture into pie shell. Freeze until firm. Yield: 6 servings.

Chocolate Almond Ricotta Pie

1¼ cups graham cracker crumbs
4 to 6 tablespoons melted butter
2 tablespoons sugar
16 ounces ricotta cheese
¾ cup sugar
1 teaspoon almond extract
1 cup toasted almonds, chilled

½ cup semisweet chocolate chips, chopped
1¼ cups whipping cream, whipped
1½ cups whipping cream
3 tablespoons sugar
1 teaspoon vanilla extract

Mix first 3 ingredients in bowl. Press into 9-inch pie plate. Combine ricotta cheese, ¾ cup sugar, almond extract, almonds, chocolate chips and whipped cream in large bowl; stir gently. Spoon into pie plate. Whip 1½ cups cream with sugar and vanilla. Pipe through pastry bag fitted with star tip onto pie. Chill overnight for best flavor. Yield: 8 servings.

Chocolate Chess Pie

1 cup sugar	1 ounce unsweetened baking
2 eggs, beaten	chocolate
Dash of salt	1 unbaked (9-inch) pie shell
1 teaspoon vanilla extract	Whipped cream
1/2 cup butter	

Combine sugar, eggs, salt and vanilla in bowl; mix well. Melt butter and chocolate in saucepan, stirring frequently. Add to sugar mixture; mix well. Pour into pie shell. Bake at 350 degrees for 25 to 30 minutes or until set. Top with whipped cream before serving. This freezes well. Yield: 8 servings.

Chocolate Chip-Rocky Road Pies

1 cup flour, sifted	2 tablespoons hot water
1/2 teaspoon baking powder	1 teaspoon vanilla extract
1/4 teaspoon salt	1/2 cup chopped nuts
1/8 teaspoon baking soda	1 cup miniature chocolate
1 cup packed brown sugar	chips
1/2 cup butter, melted	1 cup miniature marshmallows
1 egg, slightly beaten	

Sift flour, baking powder, salt and baking soda into bowl. Add mixture of brown sugar and butter; mix well. Beat egg with hot water and vanilla in small bowl. Add to flour mixture. Stir in nuts, 1/2 cup chocolate chips and 1/2 cup marshmallows. Pour into 2 greased 9-inch pie plates. Sprinkle with remaining chocolate chips and marshmallows. Bake at 350 degrees for 20 minutes. Cool before slicing. Yield: 12 servings.

Use ginger snaps, chocolate wafers, vanilla wafers
or sugar cookies to make a crumb pie crust.

Chocolate Delight Pie

³/₄ cup sugar	1 teaspoon vanilla extract
11 ounces low-fat cream cheese, softened	¹/₂ cup evaporated skim milk
	1 (8-inch) crumb pie shell
¹/₄ cup baking cocoa	1 (20-ounce) can light cherry
2 eggs	pie filling

Cream sugar and cream cheese in mixer bowl until light and fluffy. Add baking cocoa; mix well. Add eggs and vanilla; mix well. Stir in evaporated milk. Beat for 2 minutes. Pour into pie shell. Bake at 350 degrees for 35 to 40 minutes or until set. Chill, covered, in refrigerator. Top with cherry pie filling just before serving. Yield: 6 to 8 servings.

Chocolate Fudge Meringue Pie

3 tablespoons margarine, softened	1¹/₂ ounces unsweetened baking chocolate, melted
1¹/₂ cups sugar	1 cup boiling water
3 egg yolks, slightly beaten	1 baked (9-inch) pie shell
¹/₄ cup flour	1 recipe meringue

Cream margarine and sugar in double boiler over simmering water until light and fluffy. Stir in egg yolks. Add mixture of flour and chocolate; mix well. Stir in water. Heat in double boiler, stirring occasionally until mixture thickens. Pour into pie shell. Spread meringue over top, sealing to edge. Bake at 350 degrees for 15 minutes or until golden brown. Yield: 6 to 8 servings.

Cut a meringue pie with a knife dipped in
warm water to prevent ragged edges.

Chocolate Ice Cream Pie

36 vanilla wafers
1 cup evaporated milk
1 cup semisweet chocolate
chips
¼ teaspoon salt

1 cup miniature marshmallows
1 quart vanilla ice cream,
softened
½ cup pecan halves

Line bottom and side of 10-inch freezer-proof pie plate with vanilla wafers. Combine evaporated milk, chocolate chips, salt and marshmallows in heavy saucepan. Cook over medium heat until thickened and chocolate and marshmallows are melted, stirring frequently. Cool. Layer ice cream and chocolate mixture ½ at a time over wafers. Top with pecans. Freeze for 3 to 5 hours or until set. Yield: 8 to 10 servings.

Chocolate Lovers Pie

½ cup butter
1 cup flour
¼ cup chopped pecans
1 (6-ounce) package
chocolate instant pudding mix

½ cup sour cream
1 (14-ounce) can sweetened
condensed milk
1 cup milk

Cut butter into flour in bowl until crumbly. Add pecans. Press over bottom and side of 9-inch pie plate. Bake at 375 degrees until brown. Cool completely. Combine remaining ingredients in blender container. Process until smooth. Pour filling into pie shell. Chill until set. Yield: 6 to 8 servings.

To fit a crumb crust into a 9-inch pie plate,
place the crumbs into the plate and press down
with an 8-inch pie plate. The crust will
be shaped evenly between the 2 plates.

Chocolate Marshmallow Pie

8 ounces miniature
marshmallows
4 ounces German's sweet
chocolate
3/4 cup milk

1/2 teaspoon salt
1 cup whipping cream,
whipped
1/2 teaspoon vanilla extract
1 baked (9-inch) pie shell

Melt marshmallows and chocolate in double boiler over simmering water. Add milk and salt; mix well. Cool. Fold whipped cream and vanilla into marshmallow mixture. Pour into pie shell. Chill in refrigerator for 2 to 3 hours. Yield: 8 servings.

Chocolate Mousse Pie

3 cups chocolate cookie
crumbs
1/2 cup melted margarine
2 cups semisweet chocolate
chips
2 eggs
4 egg yolks, at room
temperature

2 cups whipping cream
6 tablespoons confectioners'
sugar
4 egg whites, at room
temperature
2 cups whipping cream

Combine cookie crumbs and margarine in bowl; mix well. Press over bottom and halfway up side of 10-inch springform pan. Chill for 30 minutes. Soften chocolate chips in double boiler over simmering water. Cool slightly. Add eggs; mix well. Add egg yolks; mix well. Whip 2 cups whipping cream in bowl until soft peaks form. Add confectioners' sugar; mix well. Beat egg whites in mixer bowl until stiff but not dry. Fold a small amount of whipped cream and beaten egg whites into melted chocolate. Fold in remaining whipped cream and beaten egg whites until completely incorporated. Spoon into prepared springform pan. Chill for 6 hours to overnight. Remove side of springform pan. Whip remaining 2 cups whipping cream. Spread over mousse. Yield: 10 servings.

Chocolate Raspberry Tarts

8 ounces cream cheese, softened
8 ounces semisweet chocolate chips, melted

2 tablespoons raspberry liqueur
1 (4-ounce) package graham cracker tart shells

Combine cream cheese, melted chocolate and raspberry liqueur in bowl; mix well. Spoon into graham cracker tart shells. Garnish each serving with raspberries and mint sprigs. Place on tray. Chill until serving time. Yield: 4 servings.

Chocolate Truffle Pie

1 envelope unflavored gelatin
$\frac{1}{3}$ cup cold orange juice
1 cup semisweet chocolate chips
1 teaspoon vanilla extract
2 eggs, slightly beaten

$\frac{1}{4}$ cup sugar
$1\frac{1}{2}$ cups whipping cream, whipped
1 (9-inch) chocolate crumb pie shell
Shaved chocolate

Sprinkle gelatin over orange juice in medium saucepan. Let stand for 1 minute. Cook over low heat until gelatin is dissolved, stirring constantly. Add chocolate chips. Cook until chocolate is melted, stirring frequently. Stir in vanilla. Let stand for 10 minutes or until lukewarm. Cream eggs and sugar in mixer bowl at high speed for 5 minutes or until light and fluffy. Stir in chocolate mixture. Fold in whipped cream. Pour into pie shell. Chill until set. Garnish with chocolate shavings. Yield: 8 servings.

Did you know that chocolate chips are available
in several flavors beside semisweet?
Try the milk chocolate, mint, and other choices.

Frozen Chocolate Pies

1 envelope unflavored
gelatin
2 tablespoons water
8 ounces sweet baking
chocolate
4 egg yolks
4 egg whites
1 teaspoon vanilla extract

Salt to taste
1 cup sugar
16 ounces whipped topping
1 cup chopped pecans
2 (9-inch) chocolate wafer pie
shells
2 tablespoons chopped pecans

Dissolve gelatin in water in bowl. Melt chocolate in double boiler over simmering water. Stir a small amount of chocolate into egg yolks; stir egg yolks into chocolate. Add gelatin. Cook until gelatin is dissolved, stirring constantly. Cool to room temperature. Beat egg whites with vanilla and salt in mixer bowl for 1 minute. Add sugar gradually, beating until stiff. Fold egg whites, whipped topping and 1 cup pecans gently into chocolate mixture. Spoon into pie shells; sprinkle with 2 tablespoons pecans. Freeze for 3 hours. Let stand at room temperature for 10 minutes before serving.
Yield: 16 servings.

Fudge Brownie Pie

1 unbaked (9-inch) pie shell
1 (14-ounce) can sweetened
condensed milk
1/2 cup baking mix
2 eggs, slightly beaten
1 teaspoon vanilla extract

1 cup semisweet chocolate
chips
1/4 cup margarine
1 cup chopped pecans
Ice cream

Bake pie shell at 375 degrees for 10 minutes. Remove from oven. Reduce temperature to 325 degrees. Combine condensed milk, baking mix, eggs and vanilla in mixer bowl. Melt chocolate chips and margarine in saucepan over low heat, stirring frequently. Stir into egg mixture. Beat until smooth. Stir in pecans. Pour into partially baked pie crust. Bake for 35 minutes or until set. Serve with ice cream. Yield: 6 to 8 servings.

German Chocolate Angel Pie

2 egg whites
1/8 teaspoon salt
1/8 teaspoon cream of tartar
1/2 cup sugar
1 teaspoon vanilla extract
1/2 cup finely chopped pecans

4 ounces German's sweet chocolate
3 tablespoons water
1 teaspoon vanilla extract
2 cups low-fat whipped topping

Beat egg whites with salt and cream of tartar in mixer bowl until foamy. Add sugar gradually, beating until stiff. Fold in 1 teaspoon vanilla and pecans. Spread over bottom and side of greased 8-inch pie plate. Bake at 300 degrees for 50 to 55 minutes. Cool completely. Melt chocolate with water in saucepan over low heat, stirring constantly. Add remaining 1 teaspoon vanilla; mix well. Fold in whipped topping. Pour into prepared pie shell. Chill in refrigerator for 2 hours. Yield: 8 servings.

German Chocolate Pie

4 ounces German's sweet chocolate
2 tablespoons milk
3 ounces low-fat cream cheese, softened
10 teaspoons milk
8 ounces low-fat whipped topping

1 (9-inch) graham cracker or chocolate crumb pie shell
1 kiwifruit, sliced
1/2 cup whole strawberries
1 cup blueberries

Combine chocolate and 2 tablespoons milk in saucepan. Cook over low heat until chocolate is melted, stirring frequently. Combine cream cheese, remaining 10 teaspoons milk and chocolate mixture in large bowl; mix well. Fold in whipped topping. Pour into pie shell. Chill for 4 hours. Arrange kiwifruit in flower-petal design in center of pie. Slice strawberries, reserving 1 whole berry. Arrange in overlapping ring around kiwifruit. Place ring of blueberries around strawberries. Place reserved strawberry in center of design. Chill until serving time. Yield: 8 servings.

German Mint Pie

1 1/3 cups vanilla wafer
crumbs
1/4 cup sugar
1/4 cup butter, melted
1/2 cup butter, softened
3/4 cup sugar
3 eggs

2 ounces unsweetened baking
chocolate, melted
4 ounces German's sweet
chocolate, melted
1/4 teaspoon peppermint
extract

Combine wafer crumbs, sugar and 1/4 cup melted butter in bowl; mix well. Press over bottom and side of 9-inch pie plate. Bake at 375 degrees for 5 minutes. Cream 1/2 cup butter and 3/4 cup sugar in mixer bowl until light and fluffy. Add eggs 1 at a time, beating well after each addition. Add chocolate and peppermint extract; mix well. Pour into prepared pie shell. Chill for 3 hours. Yield: 6 to 8 servings.

Heavenly Ice Cream Pie

1 1/2 cups chocolate wafer
crumbs
1/3 cup butter, melted
1 1/2 cups vanilla ice cream,
softened
1/2 cup butter, softened

1/4 cup sugar
4 ounces semisweet baking
chocolate, melted
1 1/2 teaspoons vanilla
extract
2 eggs

Combine wafer crumbs and 1/3 cup melted butter in bowl; mix well. Press over bottom and side of 9-inch pie plate. Spoon ice cream over bottom and up side of pie shell. Make well in center. Freeze. Cream softened butter and sugar in mixer bowl at medium speed until light and fluffy. Add chocolate and vanilla; mix well. Add eggs 1 at a time, beating well after each addition. Pour into shell. Freeze for 3 hours or until firm. Garnish with chocolate shavings. Let stand at room temperature for 15 minutes before serving. Yield: 8 servings.

Pecan Mocha Pie

3 ounces semisweet baking chocolate	1/2 cup evaporated milk
1 tablespoon margarine	2 teaspoons instant coffee
1 baked (9-inch) pie shell	1 tablespoon Kahlúa or Tia Maria
3/4 cup chopped pecans	1 cup chocolate chips
1 package miniature marshmallows	1 cup whipping cream, whipped
1/4 cup sugar	Chocolate curls

Melt semisweet chocolate and margarine in saucepan, mixing well. Pour into baked pie shell. Sprinkle with pecans. Melt marshmallows in saucepan over low heat. Stir in sugar, evaporated milk and instant coffee powder. Add liqueur and chocolate chips. Chill in refrigerator. Fold in whipped cream. Spread in prepared pie shell. Chill for 6 hours to overnight. Top with chocolate curls or additional whipped cream. Yield: 8 servings.

To-Die-For Chocolate Pie

1/4 cup butter	3 eggs
2 cups semisweet chocolate chips	1/4 cup flour
3/4 cup packed brown sugar	1 cup chopped walnuts
2 teaspoons instant coffee	1 1/2 cups chocolate wafer crumbs
1/4 cup water	1/4 cup butter, melted
1 teaspoon vanilla extract	

Melt 1/4 cup butter and chocolate chips in saucepan over low heat, stirring constantly. Remove from heat. Add brown sugar, instant coffee powder, water and vanilla; mix well. Stir in eggs and flour; mix well. Add walnuts. Combine chocolate wafer crumbs and 1/4 cup butter in bowl; mix well. Press over bottom and side of 9-inch pie plate. Pour filling into prepared shell. Bake at 375 degrees for 25 minutes or until set. Yield: 6 servings.

Chocolate: A Story of Success

In 1528, Hernando Cortes sent back to Spain the secret ingredient and special instructions for concocting a Native American drink called *chocolatl*, highly prized by the Aztecs, who made this beverage by first boiling crushed cocoa beans with water, then adding vanilla and spices. And Hernando thought finding gold was important.

Back home, the Spanish discovered *chocolatl* much more palatable when mixed with sugar, and thus began chocolate history as we know it. Understandably, Spain kept this new-found culinary revolution a secret from the rest of Europe for more than three-quarters of a century.

About 1606, cacao beans were imported to Italy, a more generous country, which almost immediately shared the precious commodity with neighboring France and Austria. In 1657, a Frenchman developed a method of pressing the ground beans into cakes of chocolate, and he sold his goodies in London at exorbitant prices, leaving no wonder why England had so many problems with France back then.

By 1700, the British discovered milk more compatible with chocolate than water—a monumental leap—and all across 18th century Europe, shops offering chocolate beverages became fashionable clubs. Only wealthy people could afford these places, and since chocolate, if you'll remember, did grow on trees in America, a mass migration out of Europe to the New World began at this time and didn't really slack off until about 1876, when Switzerland's Daniel Peter developed a way of blending milk, sugar, and chocolate to make milk chocolate.

From the discovery of *chocolatl*, through its pivotal role in the course of human events, across centuries of international experimentation, and emerging as a multi-cultural culmination in modern-day chocolate, it shines today like a beacon, an enduring symbol of human success and global brotherhood.

Are You "Committed" to Chocolate?

Part I
Defining Your Chocolate Relationship

We love to think of ourselves as true chocoholics, and like any other enthusiasts, we often fall short of the goals we set for ourselves. On a separate sheet of paper, record answers for each test section, honestly using the responses that come first to your mind. See pages 85 and 86 for scoring.

1. **How many times a day do you eat or drink chocolate?**
   A. not at all **B.** 1-3 times **C.** 4-6 times **D.** all day long

2. **How many items in your home are either made of chocolate or contain chocolate as a dominant flavor?**
   A. none **B.** 1-3 items **C.** 4-6 items **D.** every item

3. **When you stop at the store, how often is chocolate among the products you purchase?**
   A. never **B.** every other time **C.** 2 out of 3 times
   D. every single time

4. **How many times daily do you sneak chocolate?**

A. never B. once a day C. 2-3 times a day D. all day

5. **How often do you eat chocolate when you're alone?**

A. never B. once a week C. 2-3 times a week D. always

6. **When you wake up in the morning, how frequently do you think of chocolate before getting out of bed?**

A. never B. 2-3 times a week C. 4-6 times a week
D. every morning

7. **What amount of chocolate do you hide at work?**

A. none B. 4 oz. or less C. 5-8 oz. D. 1 lb. or more

8. **How frequently have you stolen chocolate?**

A. never B. only as a child C. only as a teen/college student
D. only when no one has been watching me

9. **When you have a box of chocolates, how often do you nibble off only the chocolate from the coated pieces and just throw the middle away?**

A. never B. seldom C. often
D. always

10. **When no other option is available, how frequently have you found yourself standing at the kitchen counter in the middle of the night eating baking chocolate squares or unsweetened chocolate powder?**

A. never B. only once C. only at the end of the month
D. every time there is no other alternative

Part II

Uncovering Your Subconscious Chocoholism

Fill in the blanks with the first response that comes to your mind.

1. White _____
2. _____ sundae
3. Hollow milk _____
4. _____ pie
5. Semisweet _____
6. _____ syrup
7. German _____ cake
8. _____ mousse
9. Swiss _____
10. _____ turtles

Part III

Determining Your Level of Commitment

Answer yes or no to each of the following questions.

1. Would you actually eat an insect if it were covered in chocolate?
2. Does the thought of eating carob make you physically nauseous?
3. Would you be unable to work in a chocolate factory and maintain your current weight and skin condition?
4. Are you unable to attend social functions without eating or drinking chocolate?

5. Do you favor chocolate over meats and vegetables?

6. Are you unable to eat just one piece (1 oz. or less) of chocolate at a sitting?

7. Have you ever had a chocolate-related traffic accident?

8. Does your consumption of chocolate affect the lives of those around you?

9. Have you ever lost a job because of chocolate?

10. When someone serves a chocolate-iced cake with non-chocolate layers, do you find yourself eating off just the icing and feeding the cake to the dog under the table?

Part IV
Interpreting Your Score

For Part I, add the following point(s) for each answer: A=0, B=1, C=2, and D=4. In Part II, add 4 for every blank marked "chocolate" and subtract 3 for those not. For Part III, add 4 for each "yes" and subtract 3 for each "no." Match your personal score to a category below.

(0-19) The Chocoholic Wanna-Be You have a dysfunctional relationship with chocolate and are taking this test because you have no life. Probably this book would be better off in the hands of someone else.

(20-39) The Chocolate Tease You merely flirt with chocolate, noticing the glaringly empty places in your life while finding yourself unable to commit to chocolate alone. You probably buy vanilla ice cream and put fruit on it.

(40-59) The Chocoholic Enabler You undoubtedly live with someone committed to chocolate, and you understand and support its power. However, you prefer coffee to hot cocoa.

(60-79) The Chocolate Enthusiast You have a fairly healthy relationship with chocolate, enjoying it when it's available without missing it when it's not. You lack a deep commitment.

(80-99) The Manic Chocoholic You struggle with strong chocolatic swings in your life. You are committed to the stuff, but you find yourself binging for a week or two, then going into denial about your real needs and desires.

(100-119) The Chocolate Fanatic You know what you want and how to get it. You have a deep-seated commitment to chocolate, and you are admired by those around you. You probably watch the commodities index and buy bulk cocoa beans low.

(120) The Quintessential Chocoholic You exemplify chocolate. You have a code, and you live by it. You do not attend functions where chocolate is unwelcome, and you share chocolate with those you love. You are truly *crazy about chocolate*.

Best-loved Chocolatisms

For centuries, the words of the great have gone down in chocolate history as credos for true followers of chocolate, providing inspiration, instilling hope and solidarity among the chosen few who take the narrow path of real commitment to chocolate as a lifestyle. As have many who have gone before you, let these words serve you along your way.

We have nothing to fear but no chocolate itself.

Chocolate soothes the savage beast.

To diet is human, but to eat chocolate is divine.

Let there be chocolate for all.

Chocolate's not just another goodie. It's a way of life.

Into every life a little chocolate must fall.

Just say "yes" to chocolate.

Chocolate. It's not just for breakfast anymore.

Following the Chocolate Path

True chocolate lovers greet their day with meditational chocolate yoga, relaxing the mind, focusing energy, and stimulating both body and soul.

First, select a form of chocolate to serve as a catalyst in your meditation. Place morsels in a bowl, put a candy bar in your shirt pocket, or whatever feels comfortable, as long as the chocolaty aroma wafts gently upward toward your face during each session. Wear loose-fitting, natural-fibre clothing, and choose an area that feels peaceful and uncluttered.

Sit barefoot on the floor in a comfortable position, preferably with your face toward the morning sun, keeping your spine as straight as possible. Experiment with positioning, trying swami-style or kneeling until you feel receptive.

Concentrate on the spot between your eyebrows and inwardly think the word "chocolate." Think it again, letting the word and all its connotations flow into your mind. Take care not to create a synthetic rhythm, and repeat "chocolate" again and again. Let the word become a focal point, or *mantra*, to which you direct all your mental energy. It is natural for other thoughts to come up as you, meditate—simply take a bite of chocolate and return to the mantra. Sustain your meditation for twenty minutes.

Once your meditation comes to a close, rotate your body into a crawling position, with your palms and knees on the floor, keeping the elbows straight. Slowly arch your back upward like a cat, gently stretching out the muscles along the spine. Then reverse the stretch by lowering your abdomen toward the floor, still keeping your elbows straight. Repeat five to ten times. Bring yourself into an upright position, eat whatever's left of the chocolate, and you're set for the day.

Metric Equivalents

Although the United States has opted to postpone converting to metric measurements, most other countries, including England and Canada, use the metric system. The following chart provides convenient approximate equivalents for allowing the use of regular kitchen measures when cooking from foreign recipes.

Volume

These metric measures are approximate benchmarks
for purposes of home food preparation.
1 milliliter = 1 cubic centimeter = 1 gram

Liquid	Dry
1 teaspoon = 5 milliliters	1 quart = 1 liter
1 tablespoon = 15 milliliters	1 ounce = 30 grams
1 fluid ounce = 30 milliliters	1 pound = 450 grams
1 cup = 250 milliliters	

Weight	Length
1 ounce = 28 grams	1 inch = 2$\frac{1}{2}$ centimeters
1 pound = 450 grams	$\frac{1}{16}$ inch = 1 millimeter

Formulas Using Conversion Factors

When approximate conversions are not accurate enough,
use these formulas to convert measures from one system to another.

Measurements	Formulas
ounces to grams:	# ounces x 28.3 = # grams
grams to ounces:	# grams x 0.035 = # ounces
pounds to grams:	# pounds x 453.6 = # grams
pounds to kilograms:	# pounds x 0.45 = # kilograms
ounces to milliliters:	# ounces x 30 = # milliliters
cups to liters:	# cups x 0.24 = # liters
inches to centimeters:	# inches x 2.54 = # centimeters
centimeters to inches:	# centimeters x 0.39 = # inches

Approximate Weight to Volume

Some ingredients which we commonly measure by volume are measured by weight in foreign recipes. Here are a few examples for easy reference.

flour, all-purpose, unsifted	1 pound = 450 grams = 3$1/2$ cups
flour, all-purpose, sifted	1 pound = 450 grams = 4 cups
sugar, granulated	1 pound = 450 grams = 2 cups
sugar, brown, packed	1 pound = 450 grams = 2$1/4$ cups
sugar, confectioners'	1 pound = 450 grams = 4 cups
sugar, confectioners', sifted	1 pound = 450 grams = 4$1/2$ cups
butter	1 pound = 450 grams = 2 cups

Temperature

Remember that foreign recipes frequently express temperatures in Centigrade rather than Fahrenheit.

Temperatures	Fahrenheit	Centigrade
room temperature	68°	20°
water boils	212°	100°
baking temperature	350°	177°
baking temperature	375°	190.5°
baking temperature	400°	204.4°
baking temperature	425°	218.3°
baking temperature	450°	232°

Use the following formulas when temperature conversions are necessary.

Centigrade degrees x $9/5$ + 32 = Fahrenheit degrees
Fahrenheit degrees - 32 x $5/9$ = Centigrade degrees

The average North American eats 11.3 pounds of chocolate each year.

American Equivalents

Measurements

1 tablespoon = 3 teaspoons	1 10^1/2 to 12-ounce can = 1^1/4 cups
2 tablespoons = 1 ounce	1 14 to 16-ounce can = 1^3/4 cups
4 tablespoons = ^{1}/4 cup	
5^1/3 tablespoons = ^{1}/3 cup	1 16 to 17-ounce can = 2 cups
8 tablespoons = ^{1}/2 cup	1 18 to 20-ounce can = 2^1/2 cups
12 tablespoons = ^{3}/4 cup	
16 tablespoons = 1 cup	1 29-ounce can = 3^1/2 cups
1 cup = 8 ounces or ^{1}/2 pint	1 46 to 51-ounce can = 5^3/4 cups
4 cups = 1 quart	
4 quarts = 1 gallon	1 6^1/2 to 7^1/2-pound can or
1 6^1/2 to 8-ounce can = 1 cup	Number 10 = 12 to 13 cups

When the recipe calls for	Use
Baking	
^{1}/2 cup butter	4 ounces
2 cups butter	1 pound
4 cups all-purpose flour	1 pound
4^1/2 to 5 cups sifted cake flour	1 pound
1 square chocolate	1 ounce
1 cup semisweet chocolate chips	6 ounces
4 cups marshmallows	1 pound
2^1/4 cups packed brown sugar	1 pound
4 cups confectioners' sugar	1 pound
2 cups granulated sugar	1 pound
Cereal–Bread	
1 cup fine dry bread crumbs	4 to 5 slices
1 cup soft bread crumbs	2 slices
1 cup small bread cubes	2 slices
1 cup fine cracker crumbs	28 saltines
1 cup fine graham cracker crumbs	15 crackers
1 cup vanilla wafer crumbs	22 wafers
1 cup crushed cornflakes	3 cups uncrushed
4 cups cooked macaroni	8 ounces uncooked
3^1/2 cups cooked rice	1 cup uncooked

When the Recipe Calls For	Use
Dairy	
1 cup shredded cheese	4 ounces
1 cup cottage cheese	8 ounces
1 cup sour cream	8 ounces
1 cup whipped cream	1/2 cup heavy cream
2/3 cup evaporated milk	1 small can
1 2/3 cups evaporated milk	1 13-ounce can
Fruit	
4 cups sliced or chopped apples	4 medium
1 cup mashed bananas	3 medium
2 cups pitted cherries	4 cups unpitted
2 1/2 cups shredded coconut	8 ounces
4 cups cranberries	1 pound
1 cup pitted dates	1 8-ounce package
1 cup candied fruit	1 8-ounce package
3 to 4 tablespoons lemon juice plus 1 tablespoon grated lemon rind	1 lemon
1/3 cup orange juice plus 2 teaspoons grated orange rind	1 orange
4 cups sliced peaches	8 medium
2 cups pitted prunes	1 12-ounce package
3 cups raisins	1 15-ounce package
Meats	
4 cups chopped cooked chicken	1 5-pound chicken
3 cups chopped cooked meat	1 pound, cooked
2 cups cooked ground meat	1 pound, cooked
Nuts	
1 cup chopped nuts	4 ounces shelled
	1 pound unshelled
Vegetables	
2 cups cooked green beans	1/2 pound fresh or 1 16-ounce can
2 1/2 cups lima beans or red beans	1 cup dried, cooked
4 cups shredded cabbage	1 pound
1 cup grated carrot	1 large
8 ounces fresh mushrooms	1 4-ounce can
1 cup chopped onion	1 large
4 cups sliced or chopped potatoes	4 medium
2 cups canned tomatoes	1 16-ounce can

Substitutions

	Instead of	Use
Baking	1 teaspoon baking powder	1/4 teaspoon baking soda plus 1/2 teaspoon cream of tartar
	1 tablespoon cornstarch (for thickening)	2 tablespoons all-purpose flour or 1 tablespoon tapioca
	1 cup sifted all-purpose flour	1 cup plus 2 tablespoons sifted cake flour
	1 cup sifted cake flour	1 cup minus 2 tablespoons sifted all-purpose flour
	1 cup dry bread crumbs	3/4 cup cracker crumbs
Dairy	1 cup buttermilk	1 cup sour milk or 1 cup yogurt
	1 cup heavy cream	3/4 cup skim milk plus 1/3 cup butter
	1 cup light cream	7/8 cup skim milk plus 3 tablespoons butter
	1 cup sour cream	7/8 cup sour milk plus 3 tablespoons butter
	1 cup sour milk	1 cup milk plus 1 tablespoon vinegar or lemon juice or 1 cup buttermilk
Seasoning	1 teaspoon allspice	1/2 teaspoon cinnamon plus 1/8 teaspoon cloves
	1 cup catsup	1 cup tomato sauce plus 1/2 cup sugar plus 2 tablespoons vinegar
	1 clove of garlic	1/8 teaspoon garlic powder or 1/8 teaspoon instant minced garlic or 3/4 teaspoon garlic salt or 5 drops of liquid garlic
	1 teaspoon Italian spice	1/4 teaspoon each oregano, basil, thyme, rosemary, plus dash of cayenne pepper
	1 teaspoon lemon juice	1/2 teaspoon vinegar
	1 tablespoon mustard	1 teaspoon dry mustard
	1 medium onion	1 tablespoon dried minced onion or 1 teaspoon onion powder
Sweet	1 1-ounce square chocolate	1/4 cup baking cocoa plus 1 teaspoon shortening
	1 2/3 ounces semisweet chocolate	1 ounce unsweetened chocolate plus 4 teaspoons granulated sugar
	1 cup honey	1 to 1 1/4 cups sugar plus 1/4 cup liquid or 1 cup corn syrup or molasses
	1 cup granulated sugar	1 cup packed brown sugar or 1 cup corn syrup, molasses or honey minus 1/4 cup liquid

Index

Chocolate, n. 1. a preparation of the seeds of cacao, often sweetened and flavored. 2. a beverage made by combining such a preparation with milk or water. 3. a candy made from such a preparation, often in combination with milk. 4. a syrup or sauce having a chocolate flavor. 5. a small, individually made piece of candy consisting of or coated with chocolate. 6. dark brown. *adj.* 7. made, flavored, or covered with chocolate. 8. having the color of chocolate.

**GREAT AMERICAN
OPPORTUNITIES**